Chronic Christian

Mark Tollefson

ISBN: 0992031923
ISBN-13: 978-0-9920319-2-3

DEDICATION

This book is dedicated to the One that empowers us to
live out the gospel in our everyday lives. May we continue
to look to God for the strength we need to live out
kingdom principles and draw people to Him.

CONTENTS

Mark Tollefson

ACKNOWLEDGMENTS

Thank you to all those that have encouraged me along the way.

CHAPTER ONE

WHY CHRONIC?

Have you ever wanted to be chronic? Would you ever think of putting the words chronic and Christian together? Whenever we use the word chronic it comes with a negative connotation and our first response is not to think of something good or something useful. We immediately think of a disease, or something that will have an adverse effect on us. We will immediately think that if something is chronic we do not want any part of the condition that it represents. In this first chapter I would like to change the way you relate to the word and introduce you to what is a better, and a definitely more positive use of the word.

The word chronic refers to something that is consistent or we could say persistent. When we refer to someone as having a chronic disease we realize that means that it is something ongoing. It is not something that just lasts for an hour but it will linger on for a period of time and possibly for their entire life. When we are talking about medical conditions there is another way to refer to them. We sometimes will refer to a condition as being acute. When something is acute it may have severe or far reaching consequences but lasts only for a brief time. They do not last for a lifetime. The symptoms will come and go but are not consistent. It is much harder to diagnose a medical condition when the symptoms are acute.

The question becomes why would we want to be chronic about our faith? The answer really is a simple one indeed. One issue with our faith is that it tends to be more acute than it is a chronic condition. Our walk with God tends to come in acute bursts of intense relationship and then go into a period of dull repetition. Many people would refer to this simply as the ups and downs of life but I would like to suggest to you that our relationship with God needs to be a chronic relationship. It has to be a relationship that affects every aspect of our lives and every day of our lives. When our walk with God is acute it is hard for a person watching to know if we are a Christian. There will of course be times when our relationship with God appears to be more intense than at other times. But our faith can be constant and we will live in the kingdom way every day, even on those days that we appear or feel like we are just going through the motions. If we let our faith become acute and allow the ebbs and flows of this life affect our walk with God we will end up with a walk that is anemic.

Our walk will be missing the abundance that Jesus came to give us. We will be lethargic in everything we do for the cause of Christ and people will not be drawn to Jesus but will actually be repulsed. If you have seen someone that is anemic you will see someone that struggles to do the most mundane of chores. It may be a struggle for them to just get up in the morning. Likewise, when we have a Christian walk that is anemic in the same way the simplest of chores like going to church will be a great hardship. Instead of waking up in the morning wondering what God will have you do that day you will wake up wondering if you can just stay and hide under the blankets.

When a person has a chronic disease it affects their whole life, as much as people with a disease like to dismiss the overall affects it still will have some effect on everything. I personally live with several chronic medical conditions and they do affect my whole life and the way I have to live. From the point I was diagnosed with these conditions there were aspects of my life that had to change to keep these conditions under control. They may never leave me but I can control some of the effects they have on my body. There may be times when it will be more difficult to follow the necessary steps to live a full life but when I go back to the prescribed steps my quality of life will increase. My quality of life is directly proportional to how well I adhere to the medical steps to control my condition. It is a daily battle to fight the diseases that afflict me.

The main condition that afflicts me is diabetes. I was diagnosed in 1997 and from that point on I had to do certain things in my life that would help to keep it under control. I am at the point now where I am on medication and have to take insulin. As a diabetic one has to watch what and how much he or she eats. It is an ongoing battle. The interesting thing about this condition is that it puts you at risk for many other medical conditions. It is much the same with a spiritual deficiency it will put you at risk for other struggles in life. Generally it is not the diabetes that will kill you it is one of the other conditions caused by the diabetes.

Anytime you need to get medical attention for anything that happens medical staff need to be aware of the fact that you are a diabetic so they will know how to respond to your current ailment in light of your chronic condition. Keep in mind I can ignore the condition and pretend that it does not affect my life and then continue to live as if I was completely healthy, but there would be consequences for that behaviour. My body would start to feel the effects and my health would further suffer until death took over. The interesting fact is that the effects would probably not be immediate. In fact it may take a while for me to even realize that my actions had done some damage to my body. I may not realize the damage until it would be too late to correct the effects. However there are certain actions, that if taken I will feel the effects at once.

Because of my condition I have to take two different injections and some oral medications. This has to happen every day of my life without exception to control the disease. Now of course I am no medical doctor but the interesting thing is that I could stop taking one of these medications at any time and carry on with my life as if everything were normal. Depending on which medication I stopped taking I may not even notice any change to my overall health. I did say that I may not notice it but that does not mean it is not affecting me in some way. Of course it will have a result but it will take time for me to realize how it is affecting me.

Because of my diabetes regular trips to the doctor and to the lab for blood tests are a must to see how my condition is progressing. If I do not go to the doctor on a regular basis I will never know if my medication needs to be adjusted to better suit where I am at now. I will just continue on my merry way thinking I am doing everything right. When in fact I may need to work on something to improve an adverse reaction that I was not aware was occurring. I need to be examined at regular intervals so I know how the disease is progressing. I hope you are getting the point here.

To be chronic in our walk with God we need to let the Spirit change us completely and we always need to be aware that we are representing God. We need to be aware that it is living the kingdom way that is our goal for life.

Matthew 6:33 tell us *"But seek first the kingdom of God and his righteousness, and all these things will be added to you"*.

This is our goal and we will talk in detail about this in the coming chapters of this book.

There has always been a discussion on how much of our lives should be affected by our faith. We have all heard those people that tell us things like, faith is a private issue or we need to separate our faith from our work life. There are Christians that believe there are two areas of their life and they are separate. One area is sacred and one is secular. When it comes to politics people tell us that a person's faith should not come into play when they are making decisions for government. Again they seem to think faith is separate from our day to day activities.

Unfortunately there are some Christians that have come to that same conclusion. When they do this they end up with a faith that works for them on Sunday but during the rest of the week it is about everything else that is happening. Their faith is on the shelf until the next Sunday. They base decisions on what is best for them and their family. They do not think about what it means to live in the kingdom during the week. These people believe that thinking about the kingdom is for Sundays only. The reality is that if we are true followers of Christ we will be unable to separate any part of our lives from our faith.

It is a fact that in today's world when we use the word Christian it can have so many different meanings. The meaning will depend on who we are talking to at the time. To some it simply means that they believe in God. To others it denotes a complete surrender to God's will. In the first century the word that was used for a follower of someone was the word disciple and it denoted something much different than the modern day usage of the word Christian. When you used the word disciple to refer to someone in the first century they knew that it meant so much more than just something you did one day a week.

A disciple is a follower. It is a person that will try to emulate whoever he is following. When a person was a disciple of a particular rabbi it meant that he submitted to the teaching of that rabbi. The rabbi was expected to challenge him in every aspect of his life. There was no area of the disciple's life that was off limits to the rabbi's teaching and it was expected that the rabbi would question the disciple on areas of the disciple's life that he thought were not coming under his teaching. Another way that we could refer to a disciple would be the term apprentice. When someone is an apprentice he looks to the one teaching him for information about every aspect of the job. He wants to learn everything about his chosen profession and if that is not his attitude he will not be very good at his chosen profession once his apprenticeship is completed.

When I talk about being a chronic Christian it means we need to wake up each morning and realize from the moment we step out of bed in the morning we are in a battle. We need to realize that the spirit is fighting the flesh and the flesh wants your Christian walk to be anemic. When a person has a chronic disease there are certain actions they have to take daily to keep that condition under control. That is what this book is all about.

Several years ago while teaching about Psalm 119 a person made a comment to me that was the start of this book. Psalm 119 is all about the word of God and how precious it is to the writer of the Psalm. It is my desire that the word of God would be that precious to us as well. One day in the Sunday School class a person made the comment that they knew they should read the Bible more than they did at the present time. Then they offered the thought that at least knowing that they had a problem was the first step. As we went up to the service I could not get this thought out of my mind. And then it came to me.

Of course this person was responding to the thought of the first step of any twelve step program. In every twelve step program the first step is realizing that you had a problem of some type. Once you recognized that there was some type of issue then you could take the necessary steps to fix the problem. So I set out to come up with a series of lessons called twelve steps to kingdom living. That is what this book is about.

As we endeavour to be chronic Christians we need to realize up front that daily we are fighting a battle with the flesh. In any military operation it is important to know who the enemy is. One of the problems in modern day warfare is that it is difficult to know exactly who the enemy is and who your friends are. The issue can become very cloudy when dealing with terrorists. Make no mistake about it we are in a battle and Satan loves to confuse Christian as to who the enemy really is.

"But I say, walk by the Spirit, and you will not gratify the desires of the flesh. For the desires of the flesh are against the Spirit, and the desires of the Spirit are against the flesh, for these are opposed to each other, to keep you from doing the things you want to do. But if you are led by the Spirit, you are not under the law." (Galatians 5:16-18)

If you are a follower of Jesus you have been given the tools you need to win this battle.

"His divine power has granted to us all things that pertain to life and godliness, through the knowledge of him who called us to his own glory and excellence, by which he has granted to us his precious and very great promises, so that through

them you may become partakers of the divine nature, having escaped from the corruption that is in the world because of sinful desire." ***(2 Peter 1:3-4)***

We need to live in the reality of this verse and live a chronic Christian life. We need to live out a faith that completely envelops our whole life. Whether we are at work, at church, socializing or interacting with our families they need to be able to recognize that there is something different about us.

At the same time we need to realize that there is a battle raging with the enemy of our soul. We need not be afraid of this battle because Jesus has given us everything we need to win the battle. But if we are unaware of the battle we will surely lose ground and fail to live abundantly as Jesus wants us to live.

Whenever a country or a group are involved in a battle they must have a specific plan. If a country goes to war without a plan they are sure to get defeated. Once you have a plan, you then have to put it into play, it is not good enough to have a plan and not use it. A country will then have to train the soldiers so they understand the steps that need to be taken to gain the victory. If a soldier does not take the necessary steps victory will be very difficult, if not impossible.

In the next chapters I will give you twelve definite steps to fight this battle successfully. If we use these steps, or we could say these battle plans, we will be able to live the kingdom way and in the process live an abundant life, and most importantly draw others to God. This needs to be the goal of our whole life. We will start off by discussing what exactly it means to live in the kingdom here on earth and then I will take you on a walk through the twelve steps to kingdom living. Let us start and take the first steps together to live life the way that Jesus wants us to live. Let us become full citizens of the kingdom. But first let us look at what kingdom living is all about.

Questions

1. What is keeping you back from being more consistent in your walk with God?
2. Do you really believe your relationship with God should permeate every area of your life? Or have you tended to compartmentalize the different parts of you life into the secular and the sacred.

Mark Tollefson

CHAPTER TWO

THE KINGDOM

What first comes to mind when I mention the kingdom of God, what is the picture that comes into your mind? If you are like most people heaven will be your initial response. Although that is not an incorrect thought to pop into a person's mind there is so much more to the kingdom then just a future place that God has promised to us, if we are His disciples. Now keep in mind there is a future kingdom to look forward to and it will be one without the consequences of sin. That is something incredible to look forward to but that is not all there is to the kingdom. The kingdom that Jesus talked so much about when He was in His earthly ministry applies to the way we live in the present and the way we will live in the future kingdom that He will establish. We need to realize that when James tells us to draw near to God and He will draw near to us it is because God is already near us now.

*"**Draw near to God, and he will draw near to you** "(James 4:8).*

There are various examples throughout scripture where we can see the nearness of God to His people. The one example we will look at here is the one of Job. Most often when we go through this book we see it as a bunch of prayers that Job and his friends pray and God hears and answers these prayers, although maybe not with the answer they were expecting. The fact of this story is that it is a compilation of prayers and conversations between friends when life is at its toughest for one of the group. The amazing part of the story is that when we hear from God near the end of the book we see that God was there all the time listening not only to their prayers but listening just as intently to their conversations. How much closer can God really get to His creation than He is right now. He is not some God that is far off and created something and now is just watching from a distance. He is a God that is interested in everything we do and say and cares passionately for us.

So just what is the kingdom that Jesus talked so much about? The kingdom is really more of a mindset or a heart attitude than it is a place. Living in the kingdom simply means to live our lives the way God originally planned. It is being led by the Spirit in every aspect of our lives. There are no areas of our lives that are not covered in the kingdom.

Some of the problem of understanding what it means to live in the kingdom, or we could say what it means to be a follower of Christ, stems from our understanding of how we were created and what we were created to be. So often I hear speakers take the account of the fall in Genesis 3 and use that passage to determine our identity. What we need to remember is that Genesis 3 is the consequence of the damage sin did to us and the world. We need to look at what God created us to be to determine what living in the kingdom entails. In order to really understand what we mean by kingdom living we need to start at the beginning.

Then God said, "Let us make man in our image, after our likeness. And let them have dominion over the fish of the sea and over the birds of the heavens and over the livestock and over all the earth and over every creeping thing that creeps on the earth." So God created man in his own image, in the image of God he created him; male and female he created them. And God blessed them. And God said to them, "Be fruitful and multiply and fill the earth and subdue it, and have dominion over the fish of the sea and over the birds of the heavens and over every living thing that moves on the earth." And God said, "Behold, I have given you every plant yielding seed that is on the face of all the earth, and every tree with seed in its fruit. You shall have them for food. And to every beast of the earth and to every

bird of the heavens and to everything that creeps on the earth, everything that has the breath of life, I have given every green plant for food." And it was so. And God saw everything that he had made, and behold, it was very good. And there was evening and there was morning, the sixth day. (Genesis 1:26-31)

Here we see God's plan and His heart for His creation. As we look at this passage we can see a couple of thoughts that correspond to kingdom living. The first lesson of importance here is the fact that we were created in the image of God. Although we have heard this many times we really need to take a moment and think about what that really means to us. We also need to see how it relates to living in the kingdom.

Some have taught that the sum total of the statement, that we were created in Gods image, was that we were given souls. This is true, but being created in God's image means so much more. And it is really much more exciting than just that. When you create something in the image of something else, you are making it resemble the original. It takes on many of the same characteristics of the original.

When we think about the characteristics of God we need to realize that we have some of those as well. Of course sin has affected how those characteristics are played out in our lives. That seems to be where the confusion comes in to this whole story. Some people assume that because sin has affected us and contaminated how we live out those characteristics that we have completely lost what it is to be made in His image.

Let us look at some ways we are made in God's image. When we talk about God being just, we need to remember the desire for justice is active in us now. We can see this trait in the fact that we have a justice system, however flawed it may be at the present time. We can also see our sense of justice in the news every day. Whenever we hear of a ruling from a court or a sentence that has been handed down by a judge this sense of justice kicks in when we think about the decision. Our usual thought pattern will be whether the sentence matched the crime. In today's world the normal response is that the sentence was far too light for the crime. We will hear on talk radio for months after the fact people calling in to bemoan the lack of justice in the country today. The opposite end of the spectrum will happen when we get a large traffic ticket. We will try to convince those we tell the story to that it was far too heavy of a fine when compared to our minor infraction.

Now I need to mention here that our sense of justice has been affected by the fall of man. When it comes to us determining if God is just we will make the mistake of applying our sense of justice onto God. We forget that our sense of justice is now damaged. But it was not intended to be that way. It only happened after sin entered the picture. It is

God that determines what is just. But this is still one of the ways we were created in God's image.

Another much over looked way that we are created in the image of God is our willingness to risk our own wellbeing for others. In John 15:13 Jesus makes this statement

"Greater love has no one than this, that someone lay down his life for his friends".

We often talk about how Jesus laid down His life for us but we do not often think of how we have this built into our character. This really amounts to the desire for us to serve each other. We were created to serve, not just God but each other and by doing so we bring glory to our father in heaven.

"In the same way, let your light shine before others, so that they may see your good works and give glory to your Father who is in heaven" (Matthew 5:16).

We can generally keep it buried deep but it is a trait that is there. In today's world when we hear of another person sacrificing his life to save another person we call that person a hero and put them on a pedestal. We believe we would never do something that noble. Although because of sin and not dying to self we are able to bury this feeling it is none the less still there. We actually see it more often than you would imagine but we manage to attribute it to something else or we just feel that person is an exception to the rule of a selfish life.

Creativity is another attribute of God that we have to some degree. Now I must state here that I am not saying that we can create something by speaking it into existence. Nor am I suggesting that we can simply will something into existence because we have created it in our mind. What I am saying is that we have a mind that likes to create and we all have it to some degree. We often look at the world around us and are amazed at the beauty of God's creation but we sometimes forget that God has instilled the desire to create in our spirits. We will look at great paintings and appreciate the creativity behind it but we generally just refer to it as being an artistic endeavor, and in some of our minds that discounts the creativity behind the work. When we look at the world around us we can clearly see that this creativity goes even deeper than you might imagine.

When you look at any job, there is some creativity going on, either directly or behind the scenes. When you go to your favourite burger place there is a creative mind behind what you are eating. Not only did someone at a point in time have to sit down and create what they thought was a better burger but they also had to create a system that would get that burger to your plate. It did not happen just by accident. If you enjoy bacon on your burger, remember that someone at a given time had to sit down and think that it might be a good idea to combine hamburger and bacon. The car you drive is a creative work no matter if it is the entry level model or the most expensive model out there. When you are performing any task the minute you start to think of a way to do it better or faster you are starting the creative process that God instilled in His creation. Again this is an area that sin has affected. Sometimes we can be very creative in ways to hurt others, but that is not the way God intended us to use this creative aspect of our lives.

This creative aspect was put in us for a reason. When God created us He did it with intention and design. Have you ever made something to eat and thought you would try throwing some stuff together just to see how it works out? Maybe you were making a dish you have made a hundred times but this time you thought you would throw in a new spice just to see how it would work in that dish. The results may have been positive or it may have ruined the meal and you had to throw it out and start over. This is not how God created us.

Psalms 139:13-16 tells us *"For you formed my inward parts; you knitted me together in my mother's womb. I praise you, for I am fearfully and wonderfully made. Wonderful are your works; my soul knows it very well. My frame was not hidden from you, when I was being made in secret, intricately woven in the depths of the earth. Your eyes saw my unformed substance; in your book were written, every one of them, the days that were formed for me, when as yet there was none of them."*

He did not just throw some stuff together and wait to see how it would work out. Instead He intentionally created us in His image so that we could bring glory to Him.

Another one of Gods characteristics that we have been given, is our capacity to love, both to give and receive love from others. The fact we are relational beings is what comes out of this capacity to love. We can see that God is a relational by the fact that the Father, Son, and Holy Spirit live in perfect relation to each other. We also know that God desires to have a relationship with His creation, us. He has gone to great lengths to accomplish this goal. We can see this desire from the following two scriptures and of course there are many others.

"And they shall be my people, and I will be their God". (Jer. 32:38)

"For God so loved the world, that he gave his only Son, that whoever believes in him should not perish but have eternal life." (John 3:16)

Let us take a look at this relationship as it was intended originally. We can see this is the early narrative of God walking and talking with Adam in the cool of the day. We find this in Genesis 3:8.

"And they heard the sound of the Lord God walking in the garden in the cool of the day, and the man and his wife hid themselves from the

presence of the Lord God among the trees of the garden."

We can see that God's intention is to have an intimate and direct relationship with His creation. It was because Adam had sinned that he was now trying to hide from God, it was not intended to be that way at all. I would imagine before sin entered the picture that Adam and Eve would have been walking with God in the garden. Can you imagine yourself walking in the cool of the evening talking about what happened in your day with God?

I live in an area that has a large beach and when I read this passage my mind goes to a hot July day. Just imagine one of those days that the daytime temperature gets up really high and by mid-afternoon the heat is at its peak. As evening starts to make its way in, the temperature starts to drop to a comfortable setting and then the breeze starts to come in off of the Lake. It is one of those times everything seems perfect. What a perfect time for a stroll along the beach either with your friends or even just by yourself. Now imagine that the sun just is beginning to set, and there you are walking in the cool of the evening, enjoying all the beauty of creation and then talking with God who is there with you. Maybe you are discussing the day's events or you are talking about what will be happening the next day. This is how God intended it from the beginning of time. And His heart for you has not changed at all.

"Jesus Christ is the same yesterday and today and forever. (Hebrews 13:8)

That is the desire He put in each and every one of us. The God of all creation, the same God that sustains everything, is interested in having this type of relationship with you. Of course, we need to remember that a problem came up that interrupted this relationship.

We are created to have a relationship, not only with God, but with others as well. If you think about it we are the happiest when we are in right relationship with God and with other people. If we think we are in right relationship with God, but we are not in a right relationship with others, we will not experience the real joy and peace that God has for us. And of course our relationships with each other are all about serving each other, not simply about making us happy.

We need to remember that when God finished creation He said it was good. There was nothing wrong with what He created. The problem only came in when sin entered the world and we became a selfish people. When you think of all the problems we face in this world they all go down to selfishness and our desire to get what we think we are due. The creative spirit goes bad when we use it to gain an advantage over others. The problem here is what sin has done to these traits that were given to us to do the good that God intended. It is how sin has affected these traits that make most people uncomfortable thinking about our innate traits as being created in God's image.

Just as Satan has infected us with the lies that he has created certain things we tend to attribute human traits to him instead of understanding who really created them. Satan created nothing but has contaminated many of God's creation. Just because we have taken God's creation and allowed sin to enter and change the way we use these traits, does not make those traits inventions of Satan. I think the best example of this is sex. God was the one that designed us, and yes that includes sex, but the world has convinced many that sex is something that Satan came up with so it is inherently bad. The fact is that God created it, but because of sin we have perverted its natural use and made it into something not intended.

Our sense of justice goes off the track when we fail to realize that it has been perverted by sin. Our sense of justice and forgiveness becomes based on what serves us best, and not what best serves God and others. Our relationship with God takes a bad and sinful turn when we make that relationship about what He can do for us and how he can meet only our selfish desires. It is the same when we take our earthly relationships and turn them into the same pattern. When we look at our spouse as an ends to a mean, that relationship becomes tainted and negative. Relationships are about serving, they are not about being served. We are to serve each other. We only need to look at Jesus' earthly ministry to see this lived out in a person's life. The idea of living in the kingdom is living in a way that redeems these characteristics and bringing them back to what God intended.

The second lesson we are to glean from this passage is that God gives us dominion over His creation. He put us in charge of this earth and all that is on the earth. This may seem like it has nothing to do with the kingdom life, but as we look a little closer we see it has everything to do with that subject. We are to live out kingdom principles while taking care of His creation. We are to take care of His creation in a way that would bring glory to the creator. We should not look at creation as being about and for us. Yes we do have the privilege of enjoying it but it was not brought into existence simply for our enjoyment. We can see this from the following passage from Colossians.

"He is the image of the invisible God, the firstborn of all creation. For by him all things were created, in heaven and on earth, visible and invisible, whether thrones or dominions or rulers or authorities-all things were created through him and for him. And he is before all things, and in him all things hold together." (Colossians 1:15-17)

It is important here to make a distinction between having dominion over, and destroying and using up the earth for our own selfish gain. To some people the fact that God has put us in charge of His creation it means we can do whatever we like with it and simply use it to gain more for ourselves and to enjoy life to its fullest. This could not be farther from the truth. What it does mean, is that we are responsible for it and are charged with taking care of it. Nurturing the earth so it can thrive, just like God has done for us. It is not about exploiting creation but is about sustaining it, and keeping it going. It is more about responsibility than it is about domination.

Just think about your life at work for a moment. At any work location you will have a certain amount of dominion over an area of your workplace. If you are a mechanic, while a car is in the shop, you have control over it. We could say that you have dominion over the car while it is in your hands. In the time you have dominion over that car it is your responsibility to make sure you take care of it and it comes out of your shop better than when it came into your shop. If that car is damaged while it is in your care you will have to answer to the owner of the vehicle, and will be responsible for the damage that was caused while you were taking care of the vehicle.

The point of this is quite simple. Since God has given us dominion over His creation we need to exercise that while living out certain kingdom principles. We need to live our lives the way God intended us to do so that we can fulfill His plan. We cannot properly take care of this world or each other without following His ways.

"And God saw everything that he had made, and behold, it was very good. And there was evening and there was morning, the sixth day. "(Genesis 1:31)

God created us this way and He said it was good. So I believe the proper statement here would be that this is what we should try to live out in our daily lives. This should be our gold standard, not the standards the world has set for us. When we look at what sin has done to us and the world we should understand the only proper and fulfilling way to live our lives is to do so under God's direction. We should realize that the way the world says we should conduct ourselves is really the way to destruction. We should not want to have anything to do with that way of life.

Next we will be looking at how Jesus came to redeem us and restore us so that we can actually live up to this high calling. With Jesus' death, burial, and resurrection we actually get to live the way He did while He was on this earth.

Questions

1. Do you truly see yourself as being made in God's image or do you more see yourself as just some one that was born with a sin nature?

2. When you understand that you are made in God's image does it change what you expect of yourself?

Chronic Christian

CHAPTER THREE

THE KINGDOM TODAY

We are now living in a world after the death, burial, and resurrection of Jesus. Why is this important? Because it changed everything. Jesus came to redeem His creation and provide a way that we could actually live our life in the way that we were intended to from the beginning. He made it possible for us to go from being selfish to being selfless. He made it possible for us to say no to sin. Not only did He make the way for us but He showed us by His life that it could actually be lived out now. We do not have to wait for heaven to live the Spirit led life, He proved that by doing it Himself.

"For we do not have a high priest who is unable to sympathize with our weaknesses, but one who in

every respect has been tempted as we are, yet without sin." (Hebrews 4:15)

It is very important for us to remember that we are able to live this way. Never let Satan lie to you and make you think that the way Jesus lived is just not possible for us to accomplish. Not only is it possible but Jesus has given us everything we need to live it out. I have talked about how we were created in the image of God and what that means for us. Next we need to look at what is expected from us. How does Jesus really expect us live in the kingdom now and what does that look like. We will take a walk through the sermon on the mount found in Matthew chapters 5, 6, and 7. Before you go any further in this book take some time to read thes scriptures for yourself.

Now that you have read them you can see that Jesus is introducing a radical way of living. It is only radical because man has been damaged by sin. Man has spent many years living for himself. Even as the Israelites lived under the Old Testament law they often missed the real idea. The law pointed out their sin and gave them a framework to live the way they had been created to live with each other. If they followed the law not only would God bless them, but it showed how they were to live with each other. It taught them what it meant to love God and love others. When Jesus came He provided a way to change our hearts so we no longer just followed rules, but we now have been changed so that we want to act like Jesus.

This is not to say that there is not a battle raging with our flesh nature. We need to wake up every morning and realize that the fact is we are in a battle. In Ephesians, Paul drives this point home and gives us a list of our armour to fight this battle. But look how he starts that passage.

"Finally, be strong in the Lord and in the strength of his might. Put on the whole armor of God, that you may be able to stand against the schemes of the devil." (Ephesians 6:10-11)

Paul is about to talk about the spiritual battle we are in. He is about to tell us about our armour. But first, he tells us that it is the Lord's strength that we fight in. It is not ours, but God's power we can rely on for victory. Then he tells us that we can stand against the devil. He does not give us armour and tell us we may be able to win. He tells us we can. There is no doubt that we can defeat the schemes of Satan. What a great promise to hold onto.

As we look at what Jesus wants for us, we need to keep the victory in mind. He never asks us to do something that we are unable to accomplish. He begins the sermon by turning what everyone had believed to be true completely upside down. It starts off with the beatitudes. This is a list of the people that are blessed. There are many sermons that will break these down individually and talk about each one. For our purposes, just look at the list as a whole. Who is blessed? What do you find all these people have in common? The fact is, it is a group of people, that at the time people would have never considered to be blessed of God. In fact many of those people listed wound have been considered to be anything but blessed. Unfortunately things have not changed much today. Jesus told them the exact opposite of what they expected.

To summarize for the sake of brevity, the one thing those people all have in common is that the only person they can rely on is God. The person that is doing well will always be tempted to rely on themselves. Jesus tells us that God is the only one that we should put our faith in. Most of us never consider it to be a blessing when life has taken us to a point where the only one we can count on or the only one that can help us is God. Jesus is telling us that this is exactly the best place to be. The reason is because He will never let us down. We can count on Him. What a start to a sermon. Imagine a pastor today starting a sermon by telling people that those who seem to have everything and to have it all together are not the ones that have everything going their way. But that is the exact message we should be hearing.

Now we move into how we should be living out our calling. I am not going to into great detail here, my intention is to give a quick overview. We will break it down into sections and discuss them.

Verses 13-16

They remind us of what our purpose is in living in the kingdom. It is not to just make us happy or content, or to live a good life, but it is to show others how great a God we serve. A friend of mine tells about how having six kids on the mission field was both a blessing but also tough. The people that they dealt with saw that, indeed they served a big God when they watched how this God took care of all of them. It is a shame today when we cannot see God in the people we are around. We are too busy giving the credit to them, or the government, or our society, instead of seeing God at work. When will we realize our help comes from the Lord, and not our jobs. Our sole purpose is to direct others to the Father so they will come into the kingdom.

Verse 17 to the end of the chapter
This is where many will break down the chapter and find some rules we can apply to our own and others lives, some rules we can judge people by. However, what Jesus is doing here is comparing the law and His Kingdom, he is telling them what it means to be led by the Spirit. Six times he uses the phrase "you have heard". In other words he is saying that the law taught you one thing but I have come to take you a step further in this process. He is not simply laying down some more rules but is introducing us to the way the Spirit will make us new creations.

He tells them he has not come to abolish the law but fulfill it. What does he mean? Do we still have to follow the law? What he means is that the law led you and showed you what righteousness is. He came that you can have His righteousness and actually live out the law in its full intent. The law controls your outside behaviours but the Spirit changes you from within.

It is interesting here how He picks six things to teach that cover all aspects of life and can be used to answer our questions about how we should act in life.

1. Murder-this covers our relationships with others both those we like and those we don't have a close relationships with. Remember most murders are committed by someone that knows the other person. He is telling us here that it is not good enough to just not do any harm to people. He will change our hearts so we will want the best for others, including our enemies. He will give us the tools we need to actually get along with others. The main way this is done is by learning to serve others instead of using people. Our relationships need to be about the other person not about what we can get out of the relationship for ourselves. He wants to change the way we interact with others before it gets to the point of murder. Jesus addresses how we can tend to look down on others and that is the start of the whole process of murder. When we start to look at others as anything but the creation of God they are we can justify treating them in a sinful way. It all starts with our heart

attitude.

2. Adultery—of course this covers our sexual relationship and our thought patterns. It teaches us how important it is when it comes to what we fill our minds with. When we look on others as a means to our own gratification we will not have relationships the way God intended us to have them. The point again here is that adultery starts in the heart. The fact is that this is where all sin starts. When we look at our relationships as gifts from God and realize we are to serve each other and not take from each other than our outward actions will show that. Jesus at one point explained to the Pharisees that it is not what goes into the man that defiles him but what comes out. (Matthew 15:11) That is because our actions show who we really are and what we believe.

3. Marriage-this of course, outside of God, is the most important relationship we will have and Jesus is driving this point home. When he contrasts the old way of easy divorce with his plan we see that marriage was intended to be for life. It was intended that we would be able to work out our differences by living the way Jesus taught us to live. At another time they ask Jesus why Moses allowed them to write a bill of divorcement. The answer that Jesus gives them sums up the kingdom principle. He told them it was only because of the hardness of their hearts that it was allowed

by Moses. This really sums up what the problems are with our marriages and all our relationships. If we would stop thinking about ourselves and put others first these relationship problems would be fixed. It is about serving others. The biggest challenge in marriage is that both people generally go into marriage to get something for themselves. Real love is about serving others not ourselves. Imagine how much better marriages would be if we served each other. The reality is that if we get our relationship with Jesus correct all our other relationships will be better.

4. Forbidding Oaths-this is talking about our relationship with the rest of the world and how they view us and our trustworthiness. At the time that Jesus spoke about this it was common to swear by different things to show that one was telling the truth. Today we will often begin a statement with the comment that we are telling them something that is true. Or we may end a statement by saying "honest". It was as though every other time we talked you cannot trust us but this time you can. This is another one of those statements that people have taken wrong. Some will use this to claim we should not swear on the Bible in court. They want to make another rule. Jesus meant so much more than just another rule. Jesus wants us to live our lives in such a way that when we make a statement we will

not have to swear to anything because people will know we are Christians so we must be telling the truth. Instead of wanting us to have to swear that we are telling the truth, Jesus wants us to live a life of integrity so people will have no doubt they can trust us.

5. Second mile—how much are we willing to sacrifice ourselves for the benefit of others. This is about dying to self and looking for ways to bless others so they will be drawn to God. When we go above and beyond what people expect from us, it says a lot to them and gives us the opportunity to share Jesus with them. At the time Jesus spoke these words any Roman solider was allowed to ask an Israelite to carry his pack for one mile. He was not allowed to ask him to bear that burden any further than that distance. It would be difficult for an Israelite to carry it even one mile because of the animosity between them and the Romans. We have Jesus here telling them to go ahead and carry it two miles. He is telling them not do just the minimum but do more than anyone would expect of you. It goes back to His comments on murder, it was not just good enough not to kill you had to go right to the heart attitude. Can you imagine what a Roman solider would think if you offered to carry his pack further. That certainly would make him stand up and take notice of these Christians. What an opportunity to share

Jesus with someone. This is what our lives needs to be marked by. We need to be known as people that will go the extra mile. People that do something because of our love for our neighbour and our love for God. What a radical way of living this would be showing.

6. Enemies—how different is our way of thinking from the worlds. Anybody can love their friends but only those that have the Spirit can love those that hate them and that is only because they understand the big picture. This is telling us how different we must be. It is again interesting how he is comparing us to the tax collectors and basically saying we must be different from the world. This way of thinking is counter culture and always has been. Most people would expect you to hate your enemy not love them. In fact they would not think any less of you for hating your enemy. But we are to have hearts of love for all including our enemy. If we can realize what the ultimate end of those people are and remember what Jesus did for us it will be a lot easier to love your enemy.

When you break down these six areas Jesus teaches us how to live in relationship with others by using kingdom principles. He takes the law and transfers it from our actions to our heart attitudes. It is not good enough to just not kill someone you need to be able to get along with those people. The Spirit changes us to make this possible. Living life in the kingdom is all about our heart attitude not only our outward actions.

Chapter 6

We have had the introduction and now Jesus moves on to the practical side of kingdom living or as we would call it, the application. It is interesting that the first half deals with doing what will please God instead of doing what looks good to other men. The whole point here was the fact that religious people were doing things so they could be seen by others but they really did not have changed hearts whereas Jesus is telling us that we need to do it privately. What is the real point here? The real point is that it is all about God and furthering the Kingdom and nothing about us and how we impress others.

And of course in the middle of this is the model prayer. Let us read it again. If you look at it as a whole what is it really saying? What it is saying is that everything is about God. The very first part is hallowed be thy name, it means to revere and separate. Next is about His Kingdom coming, not your wellbeing or your comfort but His Kingdom. We can see from this that the intention is for His kingdom to be here and now not just in some future time. Our hearts need to be about bringing His kingdom here so others can see it in action. If they see it being lived out it will be more concrete to them and more attractive. He is the one that provides your daily bread. It is He that forgives you and because of that you need to forgive others. He is the one that delivers you from Satan and his control in your life. And it ends with again repeating it is his kingdom not ours. Do you still think it is all about you?

Verse 19 talks about where your treasure is your heart will follow. Remember that everything we have here can be good but it amounts to nothing, but what we do and have in the kingdom will last forever. Where do you expend your energies? It is interesting that the next thing he talks about is the eye.

The eye is where coveting begins, it is how we see things that determine how we will react. Do we see God in what we do or do we see the world? Do we separate the sacred from the secular or do we see everything from God`s prospective? The eye is a powerful force in our bodies, and how we interpret what we see will determine who we are. We actually need to train our eye to see the things of God. It has been said that artists are more awake than the average person because they see things we don't. We need to train ourselves to see beyond the trees.

When you first come to verse 24 it seems to be out of place. But as you look at the context before and after it makes complete sense. Basically you cannot live in two kingdoms you have to make a choice. Do we serve the kingdom of this world with its material gain or do we serve the Kingdom of God and its focus on the hurting of this world? Are we serving what we see with our eyes or the God that has changed our hearts?

Then we get the great section on worry and if you tie it in with the rest of the sermon, what we get is the fact that if we let worry rule our lives we are forgetting what the kingdom is and who God is. We cannot live out our calling as citizens of the kingdom if we are worrying about the things of this life. I think we fail to realize the importance of verse 33. It is of great importance that we seek the kingdom first but what does that really mean? It means that we put God before everything and in everything, it means everything we do we do for God and the furtherance of his kingdom. It means that, as I have said before, God is not a priority in our life but it means that he is everything in our lives. He is not on a list of things to do but he is the list. He is not the peel of the orange but He is the orange.

Worry is the enemy of the Kingdom.

1. It means we are not completely trusting God.
2. It takes our minds off of the Kingdom and puts them on this world.
3. It actually makes us unhealthy and thus number 4.
4. It keeps us from doing the work of the Kingdom.
5. Worry is all about us, how often do you

worry about things that do not affect you or your family and friends.

Chapter 7
Now we move into the conclusion.

We start off with the section about judging and I believe that this is interesting because the danger that some would face when they are becoming more like Jesus is to look down on others that have not reached the same stage as they have reached. Of course to avoid this one needs to always remember that the only reason they are becoming more like Jesus is because of Him. In reality judging is just another way of elevating yourself and looking down on another. The difference between judging and correcting an erring brother would be pride. When we try to correct someone it is with the intent of making them a better person, restoring them and it is out of concern for their eternal destiny. Judging is simply trying to make them look bad and passing sentence on them. Here Jesus talks about self-examination and we will talk more about that in the twelve steps.

Verse 12 really sums up what kingdom living is about. How you treat others needs to be the way you want to be treated. This is one of those passages that even non-Christians know is right. It really makes it simple when we think like that before we act on something. It is putting yourself in the other person's place. We need to understand where the other person is at in their journey.

Then we get a warning. This relates back to the area of self-examination. Are we really on the right path and are our motives pure. How will we know? We will know by our fruit. It also talks about false teachers and again we are to know them by their fruit. The fruit we are talking about here is the fruit of the Spirit found in Galatians 5:22. It is not about the rules. In Galatians we also have the works of the flesh to contrast them with so we can examine ourselves, our teachers, and those we look up to in the faith.

With the celebrity culture we live in these days this is very important. We need to evaluate those we admire by their fruit and of course we need to evaluate ourselves the same way. It is amazing to me how many times we look up to people and when you look at the fruit of their lives it is anything but the fruit of the Spirit. We need to be careful as Christians as to who we prop up when the unsaved are seeing it. What message are they getting? We may post videos or links on our Facebook page or just endorse people in our everyday walk and although we may mean something innocent the world takes it as an endorsement of their lifestyle. We need to be careful that our liberty does not offend or hurt another's walk with God or even worse keep someone from their walk with God because they are getting the wrong signs. We need to be so in tune with the Spirit that our rights do not count. The only thing that matters is the furthering of the Kingdom.

Then he wraps up the sermon by simply stating that if you hear these words, or in our case read them and act on them you are smart. If you don't you will run into trouble. Just do it. This is the simple part of our walk. Just believe and do what he says. Why do we not do this? Why would the rest of the world want to follow us when we are not really following Jesus ourselves? We at times take out of the Word what we want to believe or what fits into what and who we think God is and then disregard the rest. Some examples of this are when in scripture we are told, be perfect, praying for the sick by the elders, and worrying just to name a few. For me, God said it, I believe it, and I will do it. That should be the cry of every Christian for everything God has said.

Later in Matthew Jesus sums up kingdom living once again for us. Jesus being asked questions and a lawyer asks Him what is the greatest commandment. The lawyer is not asking because he wants to know but he is trying to test Him. This is Jesus' response.

And he said to him, "You shall love the Lord your God with all your heart and with all your soul and with all your mind. This is the great and first commandment. And a second is like it: You shall love your neighbor as yourself. On these two commandments depend all the Law and the Prophets." (Matthew 22:37-40)

This is how we are to live in this world. This is how we are to draw people to God by living this way in a world that lives a very different life. This is why we are told we are in the world but not of this world. You cannot get anymore counter culture than when you live out these principles in the world around you. Live them at home, at work, at school, on the playground and everywhere you go.

In the next chapters I am going to give you twelve steps to live this out in your life. It is not the steps that are giving you the power to do this but they will help to keep you focused on the mission that Jesus has for us. As we follow Jesus and put these steps into practice every day you will soon see that living this out becomes our first response not our last. It is not that we will never fall but it will keep falling to a minimum. They will help you to be more intentional about your relationship with Jesus. Your walk will soon be at the forefront of your life not an afterthought.

Questions

1. After reading Matthew 5, 6 and 7 and reading this chapter do you believe you can live out the kingdom principles in your daily lives?
2. As you read this chapter and the scriptures what ways do you see that you are not living the way Jesus lived and wants us to live?
3. Do you honestly believe in your heart that living the way Jesus modeled for us will bring you the abundant life or do you still think you will be more satisfied doing it your own way?

Mark Tollefson

The Twelve Steps To Kingdom Living

1. Admit There Is A Problem

2. Faith

3. Surrender

4. Self-Examination

5. Accountability

6. Acceptance Of Who We Are

7. Willingness

8. Forgiveness

9. Stop Being Influenced By The World

10. Continue In The Apostles Doctrine

11. Maintain A Healthy Spiritual Life

12. Spread The Good News Of The Kingdom

Mark Tollefson

CHAPTER FOUR

STEP ONE
ADMIT THERE IS A PROBLEM

"Let all the house of Israel therefore know for certain that God has made him both Lord and Christ, this Jesus whom you crucified." Now when they heard this they were cut to the heart, and said to Peter and the rest of the apostles, "Brothers, what shall we do?" And Peter said to them, "Repent and be baptized every one of you in the name of Jesus Christ for the forgiveness of your sins, and you will receive the gift of the Holy Spirit. For the promise is for you and for your children and for all who are far off, everyone whom the Lord our God calls to himself." And with many other words he bore witness and continued to exhort them, saying, "Save yourselves from this crooked generation." So

those who received his word were baptized, and there were added that day about three thousand souls." (Acts 2:36-41)

Here we have a portion of Peter's sermon on the day of Pentecost. He is explaining to the people that are there who Jesus is and that He is the messiah they have been anticipating. He then ends it by telling them that they have a problem. Peter tells them that this Jesus that they crucified was made Lord and Christ by God. When they heard this they were troubled knowing they had a problem. Their response was correct upon realizing the issue at hand. They asked Peter what should they do and Peter told them to repent and be baptized and they would receive the Holy Spirit. If we read on in the chapter we will see that the ones that respond to the call of God began a new life and lived in such a radical way that the rest of society had to take notice.

When we talk about realizing that we have a problem there will be two problems that you may realize you have as you read this book. The first is the same issue that the people Peter was addressing had. They had a sin problem. They had never submitted their lives to the lordship of Jesus. In fact some of the people that were there that day were responsible for crucifying Jesus. When I make that statement we need to realize we are guilty in that as well because of our sin but these people actually were there when it happened and they may have even been the ones that shouted out "crucify Him".

So the first problem is that we are still living in our sin.

"for all have sinned and fall short of the glory of God," (Romans 3:23)

It may be that you have gone to church all your life but have never really dealt with the sin issue. You have simply gone about your life trying to be a good person and living what you consider to be a Christian life. Of course while you are trying to do this in your own strength you realize it is impossible to really do because you have not been changed and empowered by the Holy Spirit. You may have even been led in a prayer at one time by somebody and thought you had dealt with the problem. You may have asked for the forgiveness that Jesus provides but you still know deep down you are not really following Jesus. Instead you are just following a set of rules that may have been passed down to you or you have come up with yourself.

Much of the Christian church today has been sold this type of Christianity. Some refer to it as fire insurance. You think you have been prepared for the life after but you are not prepared to live the present life in the Kingdom of God. You cannot have Jesus as your saviour without making Him your Lord.

"because, if you confess with your mouth that Jesus is Lord and believe in your heart that God

raised him from the dead, you will be saved. For with the heart one believes and is justified, and with the mouth one confesses and is saved."
(Romans 10:9-10)

If you have been in church for any length of time you no doubt are familiar with this passage. This passage is used by many to tell us that all one has to do is to confess Jesus and believe in your heart and you will be saved. The fact is that if you look at this closer you will see exactly what you are confessing. This is not just some intellectual assent to a belief but instead it is teaching a commitment to a new master. It is a commitment to being a new creation in Christ. You are confessing to making Jesus your Lord.

In today's context we have lost some of what it means to have someone as your Lord. For many people today it is just a nice saying but holds no real meaning for us in our day to day life. We need to take a look at what it meant in the first century when this passage was written for you to realize that someone was your Lord.

When a person had someone as their Lord it meant their life was wrapped up in them. They had a responsibility to their lord and they were expected to be loyal only to them. It would be expected that the subject would be loyal to his lord and to no one else. Your lord had all the power over you and you were subject to his requests. Of course because you had pledged your loyalty to that lord it was expected that he would take care of his subjects and look out for you as well. We know because of the sin problem in the world this system did not always work out the way it should.

It is this kind of loyalty that Paul is talking about when it comes to Jesus. It is a total surrender to God's will. It is us dying to our own desires and us coming alive to the will of God's rule in our lives. When Jesus told us to pick up our cross and follow Him he was not just giving us some catch phrase for us to repeat He was speaking to a culture where picking up your cross meant you were giving up everything. Your life was no longer your own. This is what we are to be confessing to and nothing less than this. You cannot have Jesus as your saviour but not make Him your Lord. He must be everything to you and there can be no other lords in your life.

The Good News here is that when we do that and give up all for Him we actually do get something in return.

"Therefore, if anyone is in Christ, he is a new creation. The old has passed away; behold, the new has come." (2 Corinthians 5:17)

When we truly make Him Lord He in turn through the Spirit makes us into a new creation. Jesus gives us the ability to live this life in the way of the Kingdom of God. Through Jesus we are actually able to say no to sin. We are empowered to live out

His calling. We can actually love our neighbour as ourselves. We have the freedom to live like Jesus and the freedom to say no to the flesh because we are made alive in Him.

"Examine yourselves, to see whether you are in the faith. Test yourselves. Or do you not realize this about yourselves, that Jesus Christ is in you?- unless indeed you fail to meet the test!" *(2 Corinthians 13:5)*

Before you go any further you need to examine yourselves and see if you are in the faith. Have you actually made Jesus your Lord? Or is He just your fire insurance to try to escape hell? Is He the most important person in your life? When asking yourself the question you need to be completely honest about your answers. Everything is depending on the answer! If the answer is no then do not delay and make Him Lord of your life before you go any farther in this book.

There is a second problem we may have and we need to admit too. We may have made Jesus our Lord and it is a genuine commitment. It was not just an emotional response to a preachers call. You fully intended to make Jesus everything in your life. You have every intention of dying to yourself and serving God. But somehow you know you are not really living out your calling. You do not seem to be living out the abundant life that Jesus and the apostles talked about.

If this is you do not deny it and do not ignore the problem, it will not magically go away. You will get desensitized to the whole issue after a while and then it will not bother you at all. But that is not a positive outcome. You may even get to the point where you can rationalize the truth away. You may tell yourself that the kind of life that Jesus lived is only for the super Christians. That is precisely the lie that Satan wants you to believe.

"The thief comes only to steal and kill and destroy. I came that they may have life and have it abundantly." (John 10:10)

Satan wants you to live a defeated and dreary Christian life. He does not want you to live out your calling in Christ. Often, even the people sitting in the pew beside you do not want you to live out the full life in Christ. They want to keep you where they are in their walk with Jesus. The world will like you better if you stay in this rut as well. You will get along much better with the world in this state. But this is not the life you were created for and you know it is true no matter how much you have lied to yourself.

We need to remember that the Christian walk is a relationship with Jesus it is not a religion. We will say this often but we need to understand what this really means. Simply put to have a relationship with Jesus means that we have the opportunity to walk with Him everyday and He goes with us wherever we go in our lives. We do not have to go into a church building to spend time with Him we are with Him all day long. When our earthly relationships have a problem and they are not what they should be we need to realize that and take steps to improve them. In the same way when our relationship with the creator of the universe is not what we know it should be we need to make the necessary adjustments to make it what God intended for it to be like.

It is simply not good enough to admit there is an issue. It is not enough to sit there and say that you acknowledge you are not doing what you know is the right thing. Many times we will tell others that we know that we could do better. We know there are areas in our life that God wants to work on with us so that He can be glorified. When we know we should be doing better but do not act we are ignoring the will of God in our lives. Once He has made us realize there is an area in which we can do better, we need to respond to that and talk to Jesus about what we need to be doing. It is not pious to admit you should and could be doing better but sitting there lamenting over that fact and doing nothing to improve. A person that is in relationship with Jesus, one that has made Him their Lord will be actively seeking to improve their walk. Not because they are going to earn some points but because they desire to do the will of God. Their only real goal is to bring glory to the Father.

There is another problem you may have to admit that is affecting you right now. You may truly desire to walk in a way that The Lord wants for you. Your only life goal may honestly be to bring glory to the Father in heaven. This may be the true cry of you heart and you are sincere. The problem lies in that you sometimes are not sure of how to act it out. That is what this and the following steps are for, how to live out our calling in a world that wants us to fail and be more like them. It is important we realize here that the power is not in these steps. The power is in Jesus and He has empowered us through the Spirit.

Take a look at this passage from 2 Peter.

Simeon Peter, a servant and apostle of Jesus Christ, To those who have obtained a faith of equal standing with ours by the righteousness of our God and Savior Jesus Christ: May grace and peace be multiplied to you in the knowledge of God and of Jesus our Lord. His divine power has granted to us all things that pertain to life and godliness, through the knowledge of him who called us to his own glory and excellence, by which he has granted to us his precious and very great promises, so that through them you may become partakers of the divine nature, having escaped from the corruption that is in the world because of sinful desire. For this very reason, make every effort to supplement your faith with virtue, and virtue with knowledge, and knowledge with self-control, and self-control with steadfastness, and steadfastness with godliness, and godliness with brotherly affection, and brotherly affection with love. For if these qualities are yours and are

increasing, they keep you from being ineffective or unfruitful in the knowledge of our Lord Jesus Christ. 2 Peter 1:1-8

We can clearly see from this passage that Jesus has given all we need to live out this calling. We can also see that it is a process we are involved in for our lives. That is where these steps come into play. The power is already ours through the Spirit and now we need to put it to work in our lives. We need to provide the soil for the Holy Spirit to cultivate and to plant. That way He can provide the increase and we can live the abundant life and have the relationship that God wants for us to have with Him.

Questions

1. Take some time and examine yourself to see where you need improvement? You need to be honest with yourself and with God at this point.
2. Have there been times in your life when you realized you had a problem but did nothing to correct the issue?
3. What reasons do we usually give for not acting to correct something that is wrong?

CHAPTER 5

STEP TWO
FAITH

Every twelve step program incorporates some kind of faith into their steps. It will generally involve faith in some kind of higher power than yourself. This is intended to give you the help and resolve to complete your recovery process. When you feel you do not have the strength to make it to the end you can rely on the higher power you ascribe to in order to get you through to the end. The problem comes because they are not concerned with what that higher power is. It is only important that you have one. If your higher source of strength is a head of cabbage many of those programs would be fine with that as long as it gets you through. Of course I am sure you can see the issue with this already when it comes to kingdom living.

That is certainly not the faith I am talking about for

this step. The first difference is that it is not a faith to simply help you through the times that you cannot do it yourself. It is not just a faith in something to encourage you, although what I am talking about certainly will be of great encouragement. Many people will ask the question, will God give you more than you can handle? The answer is obviously yes He will allow many things in your life that you cannot handle. The fact is when we run into issues that we in our own strength cannot handle it simply reminds us of our need for God and His strength. But remember what Philippians tells us.

"I can do all things through him who strengthens me." (Philippians 4:13)

This was written by Paul and if there was anyone who knew what it meant to rely on the Lord's strength it was Paul. This verse was an acknowledgement that it was the strength of Jesus that allowed him to be subject to any conditions because it was God who would see him through. He knew that it was not his own resolve that made it work but it was the strength of The Lord.

This brings us to this step, we need the faith because the fact is that in our own power it is impossible to please God and live out our calling as subjects in the kingdom.

"And without faith it is impossible to please him, for whoever would draw near to God must believe

that he exists and that he rewards those who seek him" (Hebrews 11:6).

The faith we are talking about here is faith in the creator of the universe, it is faith in the One that created us, and the one that promised to help us through this life. Faith is really obedience. If we have faith it will translate into action. He promised to allow us to live a life through His Spirit that would please Him. It is knowing that without the Spirit we cannot possibly live out life in the Kingdom. We cannot live out the fruit of the Spirit without the indwelling of the Spirit.

" But the fruit of the Spirit is love, joy, peace, patience, kindness, goodness, faithfulness, gentleness, self-control; against such things there is no law." (Galatians 5:22-23).

In our own strength we may be able to live out some of this to some degree. Without the power of God it is impossible to make these a constant part of our life and our actions. Let us take a look at a few scriptures that talk about this fact.

"What shall we say then? Are we to continue in sin that grace may abound? By no means! How can we who died to sin still live in it? Do you not know that all of us who have been baptized into Christ Jesus were baptized into his death? We were buried therefore with him by baptism into death, in order that, just as Christ was raised from the dead by the glory of the Father, we too might

walk in newness of life. For if we have been united with him in a death like his, we shall certainly be united with him in a resurrection like his. We know that our old self was crucified with him in order that the body of sin might be brought to nothing, so that we would no longer be enslaved to sin. For one who has died has been set free from sin. Now if we have died with Christ, we believe that we will also live with him. We know that Christ, being raised from the dead, will never die again; death no longer has dominion over him. For the death he died he died to sin, once for all, but the life he lives he lives to God. So you also must consider yourselves dead to sin and alive to God in Christ Jesus." (Romans 6:1-11)

We can clearly see through this passage that we are dead to sin because of the death, burial, and resurrection of Jesus. It is because we have made Him Lord of our lives that we can be free from the bondage of sin. We were all born spiritually dead and had no choice but to sin because of our flesh nature. But through Jesus we have been made alive in Him so that we can follow the Spirit. You will remember in the step before this, that in 2 Peter we are told that we have been given all that is required for us to live this life the way God intended. We need to remember it is not because of us but it is because of Jesus that we are able to do this.

It is important to realize that it is not just help when times get tough that we need. We simply cannot do it in our own power. When we try to do it in our own strength we will have a life that is filled with ups and downs and highs and lows. We will be very happy when we think we are succeeding to live out kingdom principles, but the minute we realize that we cannot keep it up we will be disappointed in ourselves. We will realize that it is not possible to do it in our power so we will tend to give up and may stop trying to live it out in our day to day lives. This is exactly what Paul was talking about in Romans 7.

"For I know that nothing good dwells in me, that is, in my flesh. For I have the desire to do what is right, but not the ability to carry it out" (Romans 7:18).

Paul realized that there was no way that he could do what is right in the power of the flesh. That is why near the end of the chapter he made this claim of defeat.

"Wretched man that I am! Who will deliver me from this body of death?" (Romans 7:24)

This sounds like a man that is defeated and has given up on even trying to do what is right. This is unfortunately where a lot of Christians get stuck. They feel that it is normal to not live up to the expectations of kingdom living so they are happy living a defeated life. But this is not where Paul ends the story. God does not intend to leave us in a hopeless state. His plan all along has been to redeem and restore. We need not get stuck on this verse we need to move on to the next one.

"Thanks be to God through Jesus Christ our Lord! So then, I myself serve the law of God with my mind, but with my flesh I serve the law of sin." (Romans 7:24)

As we see God, through His son Jesus, has provided a way to get us out of the mire. He has made it possible to live in the Spirit and we can be witnesses to the world of His power and His plan. In chapter 8, Paul goes on to tell us that there is now no condemnation for those that are in Christ. In verse two of chapter 8 he tells us this,

"For the law of the Spirit of life has set you free in Christ Jesus from the law of sin and death."

What a great truth this is for those that Jesus has called and follow Him. We have been set free from the law of sin and are free to live for The Lord. We do not have to do wrong as some would have you believe. We were born dead but through the death, burial and resurrection of Jesus we have been made alive to the Spirit.

This is where our faith needs to placed. It is Jesus that will equip us to live out the kingdom lifestyle so that others will be drawn to the Father. We cannot do it on our own, and if we try to, it will be us they are drawn to not God.

"In the same way, let your light shine before others, so that they may see your good works and give glory to your Father who is in heaven." (Matthew 5:16)

Questions

1. Do you have the faith that Jesus provided all you need to live out His calling? I know your immediate answer will be yes but do your actions show this faith?
2. Why do you think we sometimes have more faith in ourselves and others that we do in God?

Chronic Christian

CHAPTER 6

STEP THREE
SURRENDER

Here we are at step three. We know we have a problem and we know where our faith needs to be placed. So what do we do next? It is important that we surrender to the will of the God and allow Him to do a work in us. A work that will make us into the people He desires. The kind of people that the world will have to take notice of and that will point towards God. It is not until we humble ourselves and give our all to Jesus that He will be able to do a great work in our lives. So what does it look like to surrender all to God?

"But whatever gain I had, I counted as loss for the sake of Christ. Indeed, I count everything as loss because of the surpassing worth of knowing Christ

Jesus my Lord. For his sake I have suffered the loss of all things and count them as rubbish, in order that I may gain Christ and be found in him, not having a righteousness of my own that comes from the law, but that which comes through faith in Christ, the righteousness from God that depends on faith-that I may know him and the power of his resurrection, and may share his sufferings, becoming like him in his death, that by any means possible I may attain the resurrection from the dead." (Philippians 3:7-11)

When you look at the verses just before the ones written here you can see what Paul has counted as loss for the sake of Christ. Paul was a respected and well educated man in his day. Paul was well trained and referred to himself as a Hebrew of all Hebrews. He had done everything that was expected of him to do as a Jew. Not only did he do those things but he excelled at them. He was head and shoulders above others in his community. If there was anyone that we may think did not need to surrender his life to Jesus it would have been him. Do you think of anyone today in the church world that you look up to and admire? You know, those people we think are the "super Christians". That would be Paul.

But here Paul tells us that all those qualifications were nothing in comparison to the riches in Christ Jesus. There was no way those credentials could make him into the man that God desired him to be. Once he had met The Lord he realized that none of those things could bring the righteousness that Jesus could provide for him. He knew that it was surrendering his life and his accomplishments to the power of the resurrection that would make him into the man God could use. Those accomplishments may have helped prepare him for surrendering to Jesus but it was The Lord and His resurrection that supplied the power. Those things in the flesh could never accomplish what the Spirit accomplished in Paul's life.

It is an amazing thing when we surrender our life to God's will what a difference it makes in everything we do. As long as we try to live out our calling in our own power we will live a life of defeat. We hold onto our own will thinking that it is what makes us strong but in fact it is what is making us weak and anemic. The very quality that the world tells us is our saving grace is in fact our eternal downfall. What a tragedy it is that so many Christians buy into the lie of the devil. It is that very thinking that landed Satan in the place he is now. He believed it was his will that was most important and it cost him everything he once was and had.

When it comes to our Christian walk we always say we want to follow Jesus but so many times we tend not to live our lives in the way He did when He was on the earth. We will wear bracelets that say "what would Jesus do" but when it comes to this issue of surrender we seem to want to do the opposite. Before we look at how Jesus surrendered I want to take a quick look at John the Baptist.

Let me set the scene here. John has been called of God to prepare the way for the coming of the Messiah. He is out in the wilderness and baptizing many people. You could say he had a following and was respected by some and hated by others. He was a celebrity of his day. People would come out to see him and be baptized by him. Then Jesus comes on the world stage. Jesus allows John to baptize him even though John knew that he was not worthy to tie the sandal of Jesus. Now Jesus has started what we would consider His earthly ministry and He is attracting attention from many people. It would be somewhat similar to an established mega church in some area, and all of a sudden another church pops up in the same area and it is starting to attract more people than the established church.

When the elders of the established church bring this to the attention of the leader of that church, what would happen in our small worldly thinking? Possibly there would be a board meeting. Maybe several meetings would take place. They would look at what they think they are doing wrong. Then they might look at what the other church is doing to attract others to their church. They may even hold some revival meetings to bring people's attention to their church. They may look at it as a competition between the two churches. Is this how John reacted?

Of course we know that John reacted quite differently to the situation. In John chapter three we are told that some of John's disciples came to him, and mentioned the fact that Jesus seemed to be getting quite a following. Maybe they thought John would come up with some kind of plan to win back disciples from Jesus. But that is not how he reacted. John explained to them that he was not the Christ. He also reminded them that a person cannot receive one thing unless it is from heaven. Then in John 3:30 we hear those words of John that we need to continue to echo as we walk through this world on our mission for Jesus.

"He must increase, but I must decrease."
(John 3:30)

Whenever we are being glorified more than God, we need to remember these words. We need to live our lives in a constant state of surrender to the king of kings. We can do nothing without Jesus. If we try to, it will not be for the right reasons.

Let us now look at how Jesus lived a life of surrender to God while He walked this earth. Both during His ministry and at the end of His earthly life he lived out this principle. We will look at Philippians and then will take a look at the prayer in the garden before the crucifixion.

"Let each of you look not only to his own interests, but also to the interests of others. Have this mind among yourselves, which is yours in Christ Jesus, who, though he was in the form of God, did not count equality with God a thing to be grasped, but emptied himself, by taking the form of a servant,

being born in the likeness of men. And being found in human form, he humbled himself by becoming obedient to the point of death, even death on a cross." (Philippians 2:4-8)

Here we have the creator of the universe coming to earth and emptying himself. It would have not been a surprise if He had come in all His glory and established His kingdom. This was actually what the Israelites were expecting to happen. But instead He humbled Himself and became like a servant and was obedient even to death. Can we say that about ourselves, or are we trying to be the one running the show. Throughout His ministry here on earth He stressed the fact that He was here to do the Father's will and apart from that He did nothing. He surrendered everything for our sake.

"So Jesus said to them, "Truly, truly, I say to you, the Son can do nothing of his own accord, but only what he sees the Father doing. For whatever the Father does, that the Son does likewise." (John 5:19)

Another great statement by Jesus! In this passage we have Jesus talking about where His authority comes from and starts it off with this verse. He is acknowledging that He does nothing outside of the Father. We need to realize this great truth of scripture, that we can do nothing apart from Jesus. Later in this passage Jesus also tells them that His glory does not come from people. If we could only get a hold of the truth that our purpose and worth only comes from Jesus we could do so much more for the kingdom. We are at times so busy trying to get the approval of men that we do not surrender to the one that will reward us in due time. We seem to be more willing to surrender to a man that we respect than to the creator of all things. We seem to be more willing to surrender our will to the boss at work than we are to surrender to the one that provided that job for us.

As we look very quickly at Jesus' life on the earth we need to look at the prayer in the garden before His crucifixion. This is where we can see the culmination of a life of surrender to God. To set the scene here we need to remember Jesus had just had His last meal with the disciples. He had washed their feet, which if we remember was the job of the lowest servant in the house. He had even washed the feet of the one that would betray Him that very night. He had just instituted the Lord's supper and He and His disciples had went to the garden so He could pray to prepare for what Jesus knew was about to happen. He retreats from the disciples about a stone's throw we are told in the gospel of Luke. It is here He stops to pray alone. His entire life on earth had built up to this moment and it is here He prays what I consider to be one of the most important prayers recorded.

Saying, "Father, if you are willing, remove this cup from me. Nevertheless, not my will, but yours, be done." (Luke 22:42)

This is truly what the Christian life is all about. Not my will but yours be done. Remember the one that is praying this prayer has the authority to lay down His life or pick it up. He could have called a legion of angels to protect Him and show His power. But at one of the toughest times of His earthly life He choose to surrender His will to that of the Father's will. By surrendering His life He gave us life. With His death, burial, and resurrection He allowed us to live out our calling. He redeemed us and all of creation by surrendering His will.

What an incredible example for us to follow. If we could only realize that by surrendering our will to His will we are given the power of the resurrection. By surrendering everything to Him we are actually gaining life not losing our life. We are made alive in Jesus. The only way to actually live our life the way that Jesus lived and expects us to live is to surrender our will to Him. There is no other way. If you try to skip this step you may be able to go on but you will never be successful in your walk with Him. You may at times be able to please your family and your friends but not Jesus. So give it up to God and allow Him to make you into the person He intended for you to be. Stop believing the lies of Satan and surrender your whole life to God and hold nothing back.

Questions

1. What are some areas of your life that you are holding back from God and keeping for you?
2. Why do we think that it is acceptable to hold back areas of our lives from God?
3. Do you look at surrendering as giving up or do you look at it as allowing the one that can help take control? Is surrender a weakness or a strength?

Chronic Christian

CHAPTER 7

STEP FOUR
SELF-EXAMINATION

A while ago I would go to the local YMCA to exercise and there I learned an important lesson while watching some of the people that were working out there. There was one young man in particular that I had noticed and he spent a lot of time on the free weights. This is the area in most gyms where at least one of the walls are covered in mirrors. There are some people that think the mirrors are there because people who workout enjoy looking at themselves. Although this may be true for a small number of people at the gym, this is not the real purpose of those mirrors.

This young man that I have mentioned was quite serious about his workout regime. He was incredibly focused and although at times I would see him talking to others, for the most part he was all business while he was at the gym. He would carry a book around and keep a record of any exercise he had done. He would use the mirrors in two different ways. When he was lifting weights he would look at himself in the mirror. There were times when he would for a few moments just stand in front of the mirror and look at himself. I very quickly realized these were not just random acts but he was involved in two activities that we need to be involved in when it comes to our Christian walk.

When he was in front of the mirror while performing some type of weight lifting he would watch himself for one very important reason. When doing any type of physical exercise it is important to be doing it correctly. Some may think that if you just pick up some weights and start lifting it will do good. The fact is that how you lift those weights, the technique that you use will determine how much benefit you get out of the exercise. The technique will also determine which part of the body will get the most benefit from your effort. It is not good enough to just say I am going to get some exercise and do it in any way you feel is good for you.

In fact doing an exercise routine wrongly may actually do you more harm than good. At the minimum it will be of little or no benefit to you. I have seen people doing repetitions of movements with very large weights. I am sure they thought they were doing a great service for their body.

Others watching may have even been impressed with the amount of weight they were using and how that person must really be in great shape. If you watched them you would have noticed that the technique they were using was completely wrong and although the weights were great, they were getting no benefit to the area they were trying to work on. I watched one person that was on a machine that is supposed to be a workout for your arms. He was using such large weights that he had to use his back to make it work. The only part of him that was really getting worked on was his back and he most likely was doing more harm than good for himself.

The opposite of that was true for the young man that was very careful to watch how he was doing his exercises. As he watched himself in the mirror he was assured that he was using the right technique. If the young man noticed an improper technique he could quickly adjust to make the most of his workout. He may not have been using the kind of weights that the man in the other example was using. He was however, getting much better benefits out of his efforts. The other person may have impressed more people but this guy knew that he was doing the right exercise in the proper way.

The other way that he used the mirror was to look at himself. Most people would see this and think to themselves that this was a very conceited young man. They would think that he must have thought very highly of himself. I do not know what he thought of himself but I do know that this was not the reason he would look at himself in that mirror. What he was doing was looking to see what effect all his work was having on his body. By doing this he could see the areas that his efforts were having the most effect on and he was also able to see the areas that he needed more work. This allowed him to concentrate on those areas of his body that in his mind were deficient. It would also allow him the opportunity to look at the results and know that he was on the right track to achieve whatever goal he had for himself. He could see that all his time and effort were paying off for him.

The last habit he had was to carry a book with him and after every different exercise he would make an entry. I would imagine that he was keeping track of how much of which exercise he had done each day. At first glance it seemed like a waste of time and maybe even a little compulsive to do such a thing. But if you take some time to think about what he was doing it made a lot of sense. By keeping track of what he did each time he was at the gym he was able to see what exercises were doing him good and he was even able to see areas he had gotten stuck at a particular level. He could determine if a particular exercise was giving the benefit he desired and if not, adjust his routine. If he had a day where he went home and he was hurting in a way that was unusual he would be able to look at the book and see what he had done differently that day and be able to correct it so that he would not keep hurting himself. I am hoping by this time you are starting to get the point.

"You hypocrite, first take the log out of your own eye, and then you will see clearly to take the speck out of your brother's eye." (Matthew 7:5)

This is a verse we love to use to tell others not to judge us. We will use it to tell people that they should not ever mention a shortcoming in our life because they also have them in their life. When we do this we miss the real weight of this passage. What Jesus is teaching here is that we need to examine ourselves before we do others. The problem He was addressing here was that many people in that day would give the outward appearance of being very spiritual and pious. Then they would look down on others they thought were not as religious as they were. They were far from God and only had an outward appearance of good. Jesus is telling them that before they judge and look down on others they ought to clean up themselves first. They needed to make their heart right with God then they would be able to genuinely help others see what they needed.

Of course nothing has changed today. We need to be constantly taking a long hard look at our own lives to see where we are missing the mark when it comes to living a Spirit led life. We do not need to feel bad when we find an area of concern in our life, God will help us correct it. What we do need to do is to see those areas that need improvement and set out to allow the Spirit to work on us and make us into the Christians that will stand out in this world. It is not good enough to see the problem and do nothing.

We also need to examine ourselves to see if those spiritual disciplines that I would hope you are involved in are actually doing you good. Or have they just become a daily exercise that is not profiting you or the kingdom. Like that young man in the gym we need to see if our Bible reading is just a habit we have. Does it actually allow you to be closer in your relationship with Jesus? Or is it something that just looks good when you tell people how much you read? Does it impress others while doing you no good at all? As we honestly examine our lives my hope is that we can see the difference our relationship with Jesus has made in our lives. If there is no difference between you and your neighbours maybe you are practising a religion and you do not really have the relationship that Jesus desires to have with you. Until we do some honest self-examination we will not know the answer. I was told a story of a young man in high school. For an assignment at school he compared his life before Christ to his life after. When we examine ourselves do we see a change in our life like that young man did.

Have you looked at yourself in the mirror lately to see if your relationship with Jesus is making you more like Him? When you look in the mirror and do some self-examination do not be like the man in James.

"For if anyone is a hearer of the word and not a doer, he is like a man who looks intently at his natural face in a mirror. For he looks at himself and goes away and at once forgets what he was like." (James 1:23-24)

When you turn away do not forget what you need to work at to become more like Jesus. This is what too many Christians do. They examine and find something but then walk away and do nothing. They know what to do but for some reason they refuse to do what is necessary to achieve the prize. If that young man in the gym looked in the mirror and kept all those records but did nothing with the information he would get no results.

As you examine yourself you need to keep in mind you are not measuring yourself against other Christians. You definitely should not be measuring yourself against the world's standards. You need to measure yourself against God's standards in the kingdom. A quick examination can be to look at Jesus' sermon found in Matthew 5, 6 and 7. How do you measure up to the kingdom life that Jesus describes in this discourse? You can also take a look at Galatians chapter 5:16-26. Check to see where you fall into this picture. Do the characteristics you exhibit fall into the actions of the flesh, or into the fruit of the Spirit? As we walk in relationship with Jesus our actions should be more and more like the fruit of the Spirit and we should be dying to the works of the flesh.

Some look at self-examination as a way to bemoan how bad they are doing in their Christian walk. The truth is really quite the opposite. As we look and see areas that need work we can rest in Jesus. It is Him that will bring about change in your life as you yield those areas to His control. Let us not be like the man in the gym never looking at how he was exercising and because of this was reaping very little benefit from his work. Instead let us be like the young man that took what he was doing very serious and then he saw the fruit of his labours. Allow God to search your heart and show you the areas of your life that are still being controlled by the flesh. Allow the Spirit to take over and enjoy the victory that only God can give you.

"Search me, O God, and know my heart! Try me and know my thoughts! And see if there be any grievous way in me, and lead me in the way everlasting!" (Psalms 139:23-24)

Questions

1. Take a look at the spiritual disciplines you are involved in. Are they actually helping you grow or just easing your conscience that you are doing something?

2. What to you tend to use more for your mirror when it comes to self-examination? Do you look more at what others think or see or do you use the example that Jesus gave us? You need to be honest when you answer this question.

Chronic Christian

CHAPTER 8

STEP FIVE
ACCOUNTABILITY

"Take care, brothers, lest there be in any of you an evil, unbelieving heart, leading you to fall away from the living God. But exhort one another every day, as long as it is called "today," that none of you may be hardened by the deceitfulness of sin." *(Hebrew 3:12-13)*

Accountability is one of those words that just the sound of it can make some people cringe. We have grown up in a world that is all about the self. We have been taught that it is nobody's business how we run our life. We are told we are the masters of what we do. If it seems good to us the world tells us to go ahead and do whatever feels right. We are generally afraid to let someone know where they are going wrong, and we are afraid to give someone permission to hold us accountable to what we say and do. This is not biblical at all.

 One reason   we are unwilling to be held accountable is fear. It may be fear that someone will find out who we actually are and not just who we pretend to be. Many of us in church today put on this act in front of people. We try to make it look like we have it all together and we may have even convinced ourselves that we do have it all together. We have also been told by the world, and the church has embraced this thinking, that our self-esteem is of the utmost importance. The problem is where we get that self-esteem from. We have bought into Satan's lie that our worth comes from us and what we have. Some believe if they have the right kind of motorcycle or the best car it represents something about them and who they are. Of course by extension they feel it tells something about what they are worth as a person. So when others hold us accountable we feel it may hurt our self-esteem.

How many of us want to willingly let others in on the struggles of our life? How you ever seen a couple that was involved in some kind of martial problems and the first thought you think is, wow I would have never thought it would have been them. This happens because instead of allowing others to speak into our lives we instead want them to think we have it all together. We are desperate for people to see us as the super Christian. Always doing the right thing, never struggling with the flesh. We need to realize we need people in our lives to be able to see the real us. Not just people that will validate everything we do. We need to be with people who will point out the issues we have. Those are really the ones that love us. The ones that always tell us that everything is ok probably do not love us enough to take a risk so we can improve our relationship with The Lord.

Is anyone doing you any good by allowing you think you are alright when they can see the problem? When we were dead in our sin, this is precisely what was happening. Before the Spirit of God brought life to us and allowed us to see the issue we thought everything was good. What really was taking place? We were on our way to an eternity without God. We were living a life that could have been so much better. Of course, because God truly loves you He showed you the issue and then He gave you the solution. So what kind of friend do you want in your corner? The one that lets you live a life that is less than it should be or the one that cares enough to challenge you to a better walk with Jesus?

We should be welcoming those who walk through this life with us. The friends that challenge us to be a better person in The Lord. If a coach of a professional sports team simply spent his time affirming all the players and never challenging them to do better he would be fired. He would never get the results the team needs to achieve. Likewise, if there is no one in our life who will hold us accountable, we will never reach the potential we have in The Lord. In fact, our Christian walk and witness will suffer because we will think everything is okay. We probably will go backwards in our Christian walk because we tend to slack off at anything that we are not being challenged about.

Another reason we are afraid to allow people to hold us accountable is that we are afraid of what they will do with the information we allow them to have. We are so used to the way the world deals with us that we fear our fellow brothers and sisters in Christ will act in the same manner. We fear that if we open ourselves up to others they will spread that information around and embarrasses us. We are not willing to take the risk. The sad reality of life is that if you are unwilling to risk anything you will gain nothing. Yes there may be times that people will not act in a way that would be appropriate. There are times we will be hurt by others. The fact is, there is too much at risk not to take the plunge. The life that we can have by living out our calling as Christians is so great that if those around us hurt us on the way it is more than worth the pain. As we improve in our Christian walk the world will notice and will be drawn to the Father. This is far too high a calling not to take the risk. Remember this is not about us it is all about God.

A few years ago I went on a diet. I was successful and lost about thirty pounds. A big part of the success was a friend at work that held me accountable in my endeavour. Although I did not have him with me on the weekend to help me along I knew that come Monday I would be seeing him again. I knew one of the first questions he would ask would be about my eating habits that past weekend. It was the knowledge of those questions that I knew would come that kept me from behaving badly when it came to my food intake. We all like to think we can do things alone, but we need to know that our brothers and sisters in Christ can be a great help. God has designed us to live in community.

What does the Bible tell us about this type of accountability? Take a look at the following scriptures. These are just a few examples.

"And let us consider how to stir up one another to love and good works, not neglecting to meet together, as is the habit of some, but encouraging one another, and all the more as you see the Day drawing near". (Hebrews 10:24-25)

"Iron sharpens iron, and one man sharpens another." (Proverbs 27:17)

"Let the word of Christ dwell in you richly, teaching and admonishing one another in all wisdom, singing psalms and hymns and spiritual songs, with thankfulness in your hearts to God." (Colossians 3:16)

These are just a few examples of the scriptural mandate to have someone that can challenge you in your walk with Jesus. We were intended to stir each other up to live a life worthy of our calling. There is an ad for the army that says be all you can be. We need to help each other be all we can be in Christ. It is Jesus that does the work in us to achieve this goal but we need to be stirring each other up to be sensitive and to be obedient to the leading of the Spirit. We are there to direct each other back to Jesus. We are to emulate Jesus not each other.

It is important to give a few cautionary notes on this subject. When we talk about scriptural accountability we cannot practice it the way that the world does. We are not there to point out to others where they are having issues because we are above them or because we have reached perfection. The tendency when someone points out something we need to work on is to look at them and see if they have it right yet before we will listen to them. This is a worldly way of looking at the situation. That person pointing it out to you may have the same issue or they may have had the same issue that God has taught them to deal with. That is why they can see it because they are walking with you, not above you. They may be the exact person to mention to you because they can empathize with you.

For the person that is holding you accountable, they need to remember that they are on this walk with you. In the example of my diet earlier one the reasons my friend was such a help was because he was on the journey with me. We are not to stir people up to good works because we have arrived at some great plateau in our lives. We do it because we love them and our desire is for them to experience the abundant life that Jesus provides for us. Remember, as we remove the log that is our eye we will be better able to remove the speck in our brothers eye. This is not some kind of self-righteous act of the perfect helping the less fortunate. It is two people walking and doing life together. It is two people growing in their relationship with Jesus together. It should be an act that is mutually beneficial. It should be something that builds up the kingdom. It is not tearing someone down. As the world sees us working together in this process they will see people that genuinely care about each other's wellbeing and want nothing but the best for each other.

Questions
1. If you do not have someone that you are accountable to, what are the reasons for not having a person like this in your life?
2. Do you have someone that is accountable to you and why is this arrangement easier?
3. What scares you most about having an accountability partner?

Chronic Christian

CHAPTER NINE

STEP SIX
ACCEPTANCE OF WHO WE ARE

Who we believe we are will affect all of our actions and feelings. It will determine our self-worth. It will affect what we try to accomplish or how fast we give up on something we are doing. It will determine how we react to other people. Both in our reaction to how they treat us, and how we see who they are and what they are worth. It will set the standard for how we view God and what we think we can accomplish through Him. Simply put, who we believe we are will determine pretty well everything about us.

There are many people in the world today that have been told that they were somehow substandard in somebodies estimation and it has affected their entire life. When we read the newspaper and we see how people are behaving, you can imagine that somewhere in their past is a story of another person making them believe a lie. There have been stories of people doing what we would term unspeakable things to others. Many times those peoples deeds were started at a point when someone somehow convinced them that they were flawed. They had been convinced that they were destined to do those things because they were bad. They thought they were not worthy to do anything better. We have people that have spent their whole lives not knowing who they are in God. Their actions have demonstrated this and worse they have sought validation from many other sources. Sources that were actually very destructive to them and those around them.

It is unfortunate that so many Christians do not completely understand what it means to be in Christ. Due to that misunderstanding they go around living a defeated life. They feel that they can do no better than what they are doing right now and that there is no chance of them improving in their walk with God. There are satisfied with less than God intended for them. They seemed to have accepted the lie that they have no choice but to sin and live the same as the rest of world lives. It is sad to see that those that are called by God will accept the lies that the devil has told them.

There are stories about people that live on the street that actually do not have to be there for financial reasons. They may actually have a lot of money sitting somewhere that they could use but for some reason they never touch the money. It could be for different reasons, it may be because of mental health issues or they may just prefer to live this way. Or it could be someone that comes from a wealthy family that simply choses to live in a different way and never accesses the wealth that is available to them.

The question here is who we become when we are in Christ? The first way to answer that question is to state who we are not once we have made Jesus our Lord. We are not some poor miserable creature that will barely make it to heaven. We are also not just a sinner saved by grace. These are but two ways some Christian refer to themselves. These both are far from the truth when it comes to those that follow Jesus. People also couple these two statements together. They will add that because of those two statements they have no choice but to sin once in a while. You can see that by believing these kinds of lies about Christians they will fail to live a life that is attractive to those around them. How can God be glorified when according to these two statements He is even unable to redeem and restore His creation. These are lies that Satan loves us to believe and they are statements that grieve the heart of God.

God has done so much more for us and turned us into new creations, saints and His family.

"From now on, therefore, we regard no one

according to the flesh. Even though we once regarded Christ according to the flesh, we regard him thus no longer. Therefore, if anyone is in Christ, he is a new creation. The old has passed away; behold, the new has come." (2 Corinthians 5:16-17)

Once we have made Jesus our Lord we are made into something new by the Spirit of God. As the verse says the old has passed away. It is not like putting a patch on an old pair of jeans just to make them last for a bit longer. In fact in Matthew 9 Jesus tells us a parable about just that. We are not just some miserable sinner that has added Jesus to his life to make it more bearable. We have taken on and been given a new identity. We are no longer the same, we have been given the ability to live out our calling in the Kingdom. He has enabled us to live our life and exhibit the fruit of the Spirit. We are no longer subject to the flesh. We now are free in Christ to make a choice. Just look at what Paul says about this.

"There is therefore now no condemnation for those who are in Christ Jesus. For the law of the Spirit of life has set you free in Christ Jesus from the law of sin and death. For God has done what the law, weakened by the flesh, could not do. By sending his own Son in the likeness of sinful flesh and for sin, he condemned sin in the flesh, in order that the righteous requirement of the law might be fulfilled in us, who walk not according to the flesh but according to the Spirit. For those

who live according to the flesh set their minds on the things of the flesh, but those who live according to the Spirit set their minds on the things of the Spirit. "For to set the mind on the flesh is death, but to set the mind on the Spirit is life and peace." (Romans 8:1-6)

He has freed us from slavery to sin, and allowed us to follow Him. Of course we need to remember that there is a daily battle being fought with the flesh and that is the purpose of these twelve steps. It is to give you a victory strategy to win. Although we need to be aware of the daily battle we also need to remember what God has done for us and to us. He gave us what is necessary to be successful in the battle. We are not destined to failure and to keep sinning. We are able to overcome the world through Jesus.

"I have said these things to you, that in me you may have peace. In the world you will have tribulation. But take heart; I have overcome the world." (John 16:33)

Many Christians have trouble accepting the fact that they are now the saints of God. This stems from Satan's lie and what we have decided it means to be a saint. We tend to look at being a saint as something you earn and work towards, thus it is because of your efforts. This is not what scripture talks about when referring to us as saints. We are saints based on what Jesus has done, not based on our own efforts. It is not because of who we are but it is because of whose we are. When we give our lives to Jesus we put on His righteousness. It is because of Him and His great mercy that we are now the saints of God.

"For we are his workmanship, created in Christ Jesus for good works, which God prepared beforehand, that we should walk in them." (Ephesians 2:10)

In many of Paul's letters he refers to those whom he is writing to as saints. We need to remember that some of those letters were sent to correct errors in those churches. In one of the letters to the Corinthians he tells them that one of the issues they were having was so bad it was not even normal for unbelievers. Yet he still opened the letter by calling them saints. That is because that title is based on the work of Jesus in our life not on how good we have become.

"For all who are led by the Spirit of God are sons of God. For you did not receive the spirit of slavery to fall back into fear, but you have received the Spirit of adoption as sons, by whom we cry, "Abba! Father!" (Romans 8:14)

We have through the death, burial and resurrection of Jesus become part of His family. Have you ever met anyone that was ashamed of being part of their family? There are some that do not want to be associated with their particular family name. Then of course there is the opposite end of that and some are extremely proud to be part of their family and want everyone to know they are part of that family. There are some family names that the mere mention that you are part of that family will allow you special privileges. If you have a particular family name it may be expected of you to do things so that you can live up to that heritage. For you not to do so would be considered unusual.

Now take a moment to contemplate the fact that you have been adopted into the family of the creator of the universe. Once we accept the fact that we are part of the family of God it has to change the way we view ourselves and our actions. No longer will we feel that we are unworthy or unloved. You will realize that your actions will reflect on the whole family. You now have a higher standard to live up to and God has given you the power to do just that. When others in this world look down on you just remember that you are a child of the king of kings. When you are part of an earthly family that has wealth and privilege they will generally provide you with all you need to succeed in this world. They will provide you with the best of everything this world can offer. Being part of that family will usually get you into the best of schools. The only thing that will hold you back is you.

In a similar way God has given you everything you need to live in the kingdom. He has given you what you need to fight temptation. By being adopted into His family we are given the power to operate in the kingdom of God. We are given the power to love others and put them first. We have been given the ability to die to our flesh.

When you understand and accept who you are in Christ it must change your outlook. When you realize you can refer to God as Abba Father you will feel truly loved and cared for. You will do everything to live up to your calling regardless of the price. Instead of trying to get away with the minimal effort required you will look for ways to please Him more and more. You will look for ways to invite others into this great family. When we truly understand our identity and understand we are new creations our lives will show it and we will be living the abundant life that Jesus told us He came to give.

Questions
1. Before you read this chapter who did you think you were? Now that you have read the chapter who do you believe you are now?
2. Why is it easier for us to believe we are miserable sinners instead of the saints Jesus has made us into?
3. How can you remind yourself each day that you are a new creation and part of God's family?

Mark Tollefson

CHAPTER TEN

STEP SEVEN
WILLINGNESS

You have heard the saying " you can lead a horse to water but you can't make him drink". Have you ever tried to get a child to eat something they really did not like? Have you ever been in a meeting trying to convince people of something that they were just unwilling to accept? Have you ever tried to accomplish a task that you did not really want to finish? How hard is it for a person to get up in the morning and go into a job that they really do not like? Have you ever tried to convince your spouse to go somewhere they just did not want to go? You can guilt them or manipulate them into going but it just will not be the same as it would be, if their whole heart was in to the outing. Churches and religion can force or manipulate or even guilt their adherents to toe the line and do things that they feel would please God. But there needs to be a willingness on the part of the follower of Jesus to make it count and to have it really change the person's heart. As Jesus told the Pharisees their outward actions showed one thing but their hearts were far from God.

There are many people living the Christian life in this manner. They are trying to be successful but they really would rather be living life in a different manner. They are not really willing participants in the kingdom. They may only be in this kingdom for something they can get out of it and have not been actually changed by the Spirit. It seems that everything they do is a big sacrifice for them. Instead of telling others that they have the privilege of being led by the Spirit. They seem to just do it because they believe they have to do things that way and they have no other choice.

There are some Christians that believe that if they just pray enough or in the right way, everything will change. If they are struggling with a particular area in their life they will pray and just expect God to wave some kind of wand and the temptation will disappear. Now we have discussed earlier that God does empower us to live this life but that is not done by taking away every temptation. In fact as you recall Jesus led a life without sin but He was still tempted by the devil. He was able of course to have victory over those temptations. It wasn't that He was never tempted, it was that He used the power He had to overcome temptation. We will be fighting a battle with the flesh daily and God will not take us out of it but He will empower us to die to ourselves daily. This is where willingness comes into the picture.

We need to be willing to live out our lives in light of what God has done for us. Before we look at some biblical examples take a moment to look at your life and anything you have accomplished. It will quickly become apparent how this principle plays itself out. If you have finished any type of schooling you know that it took a willingness for you do achieve that goal. You may have been willing to endure the hardships of gaining that education for any number of reasons, but you had to be willing to finish. We have the choice and we have to make the right choice. People drop out of school because they are not willing to stay the course to completion. It is a choice they have made. Do not under estimate how important our choices are in regards to our Christian walk. We need to be willing to do whatever it takes to bring glory to the Father.

I would like to take a look at how Paul put this step into practice in his life.

"But whatever gain I had, I counted as loss for the sake of Christ. Indeed, I count everything as

loss because of the surpassing worth of knowing Christ Jesus my Lord. For his sake I have suffered the loss of all things and count them as rubbish, in order that I may gain Christ." (Philippians 3:7-8)

In this passage Paul talks about his credentials as a Jew. He was well qualified to be a leader in the community and by their standards he was a very righteous man. Yet he is willingly counting all those things as loss for the sake of the gospel. He is willingly giving up his rights in order to follow Jesus and be led by the Spirit. It is interesting, because they already did not really amount to anything by God's standard but it is not until Paul is willing to accept that fact that The Lord was able to make better use of his testimony and work through him.

As long as we feel that we have accomplished something on our own we will never be able to see what God can and will do through us. We need to be willing to die to our own desires to allow God to shine through us and draw others to Himself. In the same way we need to make a conscious decision to react to others the way Jesus commands us to do in the sermon on the mount. We need to be willing to do it his way even if it is difficult. He will change our heart and give us the desire to please Him but we need to wake up every day and decide to do life His way not ours and He will empower us to achieve the goal of being more like Him.

"Now therefore fear the LORD and serve him in

sincerity and in faithfulness. Put away the gods that your fathers served beyond the River and in Egypt, and serve the LORD. And if it is evil in your eyes to serve the LORD, choose this day whom you will serve, whether the gods your fathers served in the region beyond the River, or the gods of the Amorites in whose land you dwell. But as for me and my house, we will serve the LORD." (Joshua 24:14-15)

This is Joshua's final address to the people of Israel. He has gone through some of the history of his people and spoke of what God has done for them. He then comes to this part of the address and he challenges them. They have a choice, if they think it is better to serve other gods then they are free to do just that. However if they realize the greatness of the one true God they can chose to serve Him and receive His blessings.

Their decision will not change God and His sovereignty but it will affect them and their access to God's blessings. All throughout the Old Testament the people are given a choice of what they are willing to do with God. Their willingness or unwillingness will have a profound effect on them. They can chose to follow God and experience blessings or they can chose to live life their way and experience the curses of God. It was their willingness to do one or the other that unlocked the door to what their future would be like.

In the same way we are faced with a choice in our lives. The first choice is whether or not we will follow Jesus at all. The next question is are we willing to live it out His way and experience the abundant life that Jesus came to give? Or will we try to do it our way and live a defeated Christian life?

"I appeal to you therefore, brothers, by the mercies of God, to present your bodies as a living sacrifice, holy and acceptable to God, which is your spiritual worship. Do not be conformed to this world, but be transformed by the renewal of your mind, that by testing you may discern what is the will of God, what is good and acceptable and perfect." (Romans 12:12)

Paul has written this letter explaining what Christ has done for us. He gets to this part of the letter and tell us that because of what was explained earlier in the letter this should be our response. This is where our choice comes into play. Whatever our response is it will not change what God has done but here again it will change how we live it out in our day to day lives. It requires a response on our part to live it. We need to be willing to submit to the leading of the Spirit. If we look in chapter four of Ephesians we can see a similar thought as we have here.

"Therefore, having put away falsehood, let each one of you speak the truth with his neighbor, for we are members one of another. Be angry and do

not sin; do not let the sun go down on your anger, and give no opportunity to the devil. Let the thief no longer steal, but rather let him labor, doing honest work with his own hands, so that he may have something to share with anyone in need. Let no corrupting talk come out of your mouths, but only such as is good for building up, as fits the occasion, that it may give grace to those who hear. And do not grieve the Holy Spirit of God, by whom you were sealed for the day of redemption. Let all bitterness and wrath and anger and clamor and slander be put away from you, along with all malice. Be kind to one another, tenderhearted, forgiving one another, as God in Christ forgave you." (Ephesians 4:25-32)

As you can see there is a choice here and again Paul is giving us what our response should be. He is not telling them that this is what God is now going to force you to do because you follow Him. Instead the concept here is that God will empower you to be able to live out. But there still has to be a willingness on our part to succeed. When we think God will make it so we cannot fall into sin we really do not quite understand what He has done for us. To simplify it here, with the death, burial and resurrection of Jesus and the imparting of the Holy Spirit we are given the ability to say no to sin. We are able to make the right choices, whereas before, we were slaves to sin. He has changed us so that we will actually want to do what is right and pleasing to The Lord. He has provided us with choice.

We need to get up every day and make the choice to live for Him. We need to be willing to live out the kingdom principles in our lives daily. When we are willing to be obedient to Jesus we will discover a life that is fulfilling and satisfying in a way the world can never provide. When we are willing God will empower us to live it out in our day to day life. If you are unwilling to take the steps to live out our calling you will miss out on the greatest blessings that one can have in this life.

Questions
1. What are you most willing to do in life?
2. What do you find most difficult to be willing to do in your life?
3. List some reasons we should be willing to live out the kingdom principles that Jesus taught us.

Chronic Christian

CHAPTER ELEVEN

STEP EIGHT

FORGIVENESS

Most twelve step programs involve a step of forgiveness. It is generally aimed at you making amends to those that you have hurt because of your problem. There is however more to the subject than just making amends to those we have hurt along the way. The forgiveness I want to address is three fold. We need to accept, administer and ask forgiveness.

Have you ever met anyone that is so devastated by something they have done that they are not able to carry on with their life in a healthy way? They may have done something to another person and even though that person has forgiven them they are riddled with guilt. They may have even made restitution to the person but they still cannot forgive themselves. There are people that realize the actions they have taken have not pleased God and they feel that God could never forgive them for the horrendous things they have done. We need to be in a place that we can accept the forgiveness of others and most importantly the forgiveness that God has offered us when we humble ourselves and follow Jesus.

"as far as the east is from the west, so far does he remove our transgressions from us'. (Psalms 103:12)

"my little children, I am writing these things to you so that you may not sin. But if anyone does sin, we have an advocate with the Father, Jesus Christ the righteous. He is the propitiation for our sins, and not for ours only but also for the sins of the whole world." (1 John 2:1-2)

As we look at these scriptures we need to believe them and accept them as truth. Anything else that we believe about forgiveness that does not line up with scripture is a lie from Satan. Satan does not want you to accept these truths because he knows that they bring you freedom in Christ. The devil wants us to live a defeated life, Jesus tells us that Satan comes to seek and destroy (John 10:10). Why would we believe the one that wants to destroy us instead of holding on to the truth of God. God does not want you to live your life in guilt He wants to restore you.

"godly grief produces a repentance that leads to salvation without regret, whereas worldly grief produces death." (2 Corinthians 7:10)

This is what God wants for you. He wants conviction to come on you so that you can be restored to Him. He wants us to live in victory over our mistakes because of what Jesus has done for us. The above passage was written by Paul to the Corinthian church. He had written them two letters to correct errors that had come up in the church. He explains to them that it was not to lead them to a life of guilt and regret. But it was to lead them to realize the error of their ways so they could be restored. He mentions these things to bring them back and lift them up, no to tear them down.

The reason we have such a difficult time with this concept is because of the flesh nature. Generally speaking when those that are not living the Spirit led life bring up wrongs people have done is because they want to knock them down. Many times it is because people want to see you suffer for what you have done. They also like to feel superior to you because they think, "at least I am not that bad". We need to be careful we do not put the works of the flesh onto God and assume that He is acting in the same manner. He does not live in the flesh and He does not have the works of the flesh. He is the perfect example of the fruit of the Spirit. This of course goes back to our concept of God and who He is. You need to review Galatians 5:16-26. This passage contrasts the fruit of the Spirit with the works of the flesh. Whenever we find ourselves ascribing the works of the flesh to God we need to stop immediately and realize those do not apply to Him.

We need to start accepting what God has told us in scripture and stop adding rules to it that God never added. Stop mixing the lies of Satan in with the truth of God. God has removed our sins as far as the east is from the west. Think about that for a minute. If you were to walk straight north and keep going you would eventually be walking south. The interesting thought about this passage is that if you start walking east and keep going you will never at any time be going west. You will always be going east until you actually change direction. That is what God has done with our transgressions, He has removed them forever.

Next we need to administer forgiveness. There are verses that teach us that we have no choice but to forgive others if we are being led by the Spirit. It is not an option once God has forgiven us. Jesus even tells us that it is a never ending process. There is no point at which we can say that we have forgiven someone enough and we do not have to forgive anymore. You can take a look at the following scriptures about forgiveness yourself because I am going on the premise that we all know we have no choice but to forgive others no matter what they have done. I do want to look at why it is important to forgive so that we can live the kingdom life.

- Matthew 6:14-15
- Matthew 18:2-35
- Colossians 3:12-13
- Mark 11:22-35

Let us take a look at why it is necessary for us to forgive to live out our calling as Jesus' disciples.

"See to it that no one fails to obtain the grace of God; that no "root of bitterness" springs up and causes trouble, and by it many become defiled;" (Hebrews 12:15)

This passage starts out at the beginning of chapter twelve with the word, therefore. The writer is saying that because of the what Jesus has done and who He is, this is how you should live your life. This is a response to what The Lord has done for you and me. The part of this passage I will zero in on is the root of bitterness and how it causes trouble when we refuse to forgive others for what they may have done. It is amazing how much an unforgiving spirit can damage our Christian walk. When we hold a grudge against one person the effects stretch to many other people in our lives.

As I showed earlier we can at times ascribe human characteristics and behaviours on God. Because we see those around us acting in certain ways there is a temptation to think that God operates in the same way. Similarly, we will at times think that everyone in our life is treating us the same way that someone we are holding a grudge against is doing. Because we have not released that person we tend to look at others with the same lens. We tend to look at all people with suspicion because we have not dealt with the first problem. It does not allow us to have relationships with other people in the way we were intended to live with them.

The root of bitterness will grow in all other areas of our lives. It will also affect our relationship with God. We are told in scripture that our prayer life will be hindered if we are not following God's way of life. We cannot hold back forgiveness from another and expect that our relationship with God will be normal. In fact in Matthew 7 we are told that if we do not forgive others God will not forgive us.

"And do not grieve the Holy Spirit of God, by whom you were sealed for the day of redemption. Let all bitterness and wrath and anger and clamor and slander be put away from you, along with all malice. Be kind to one another, tenderhearted, forgiving one another, as God in Christ forgave you." (Ephesians 4:30-32)

In this passage we are told straight out by Paul that when we do not forgive others we are grieving the Holy Spirit. How can our relationship with Jesus be at its best if we are grieving the Holy Spirit? If you look at this verse closely you can see the things that not forgiving one another brings into your life. If you look at the issue and look at your life you will see how this plays out.

First there is the offence that someone does to us. We do not forgive so we are no longer tender-hearted toward them and maybe even toward others. Then the feelings you have for this person will be ones that wish them harm. We will tell ourselves at that point it is really for their own good. Then as we hang on to that anger we will become very bitter and every time we think or see that person it will be like it just happened to us. We will be consumed by it and it will affect all areas of our life. We will lie to ourselves and say that it is under control but we are really only fooling ourselves. Or should I say that Satan is deceiving us. Everything that happens to us will be related to that wrong that we think we have a right to hang on to. That is the root of bitterness.

I have met people in my life that are in exactly that spot. Their lives have been consumed by the times they feel they were not treated right in life. When you listen to people trapped in this place tell the story of what happened it is like they are reliving it all over again. The incident may have happened thirty years ago. When they retell the story you can see how it is getting them upset all over again in just the same way it did on the day that it happened. Sometimes there will be another news story or television show and it will remind them of the event and it will be in the fore front all over again. What an awful way to go through life. The sad part is that the person who committed the original wrong has probably long since forgotten the incident. Do we really think we can live in the kingdom with this kind of bitterness in our heart?

The last part of forgiveness we need to look at is asking for forgiveness. The first person we need to seek that forgiveness from is God. Of course if we never have had a relationship with Jesus we need to start at the beginning. We need to make Him lord of our lives and ask for and accept the forgiveness that He offers for our rejection of Him. We need to allow Jesus to make us into the new creation we have been talking about in this book. The new creation that allows us to live out this life that he has for us.

If we have already made Jesus our Lord and we are in relationship with Him there may be times when we drop the ball. There will be times in our lives that we just do not act in a way that is in keeping with the kingdom lifestyle. It is on these occasions we need to be quick to admit our wrong and ask Him for forgiveness. The great promise is that He has made provision for this and promises to give forgiveness in these situations. Look at what 1 John has to say about this.

"If we confess our sins, he is faithful and just to forgive us our sins and to cleanse us from all unrighteousness." (1 John 1:9)

Of course we also have to ask forgiveness from those we have offended. We need to be quick to act on this when the Spirit leads us to that point. We need to go to the person as soon as you can and ask for their forgiveness. If we put it off three things will happen. The first is that we will spend time rationalizing why we do not need to apologize. As we do this it will become more and more difficult to actually forgive when we do decide to follow the leading of the Holy Spirit. We may even convince ourselves that we do not even need to apologize and that the Spirit was wrong. Of course we will not verbalize it that way but this is what we are saying by our actions. We are saying we know better than God.

This is when the second problem can occur. By ignoring the leading of the Spirit we will get to a point we will not even recognize His leading. And if we do still experience His leading we will be constantly second guessing God. Again you may think you are just being sure but what you are really doing is saying "wait a minute God, I may have a better plan". If we are not being led by the Spirit the only other option is being led by the world and that is not a good option. Of course if we are not following the leading of the Holy Spirit, then we are living with sin.

The third problem that delaying will create is it will make it harder to ask forgiveness when you do decide to do so because that time will not only have affected you as we have already mentioned. Because of greater time lapsing the person you have offended may have had a root of bitterness growing up in them. This may have caused damage already and now there is more of an issue than when it first began. For you to actually go to the person it will be much harder. Take a moment and think of the times in your life when you have had to apologize to another person.

How easy was it if the moment the offence happened you told them you were sorry? How hard was it when a great amount of time had passed? Growing up they used to tell us to keep our accounts short when it came to God. The same is true for each other. Do not give time for Satan to put thoughts into our minds or the minds of those we have hurt. Do not give time for there to be divisions in the body of Christ. Do not allow the root of bitterness to grow.

Questions
1. Which is harder for you personally, to accept, administer or ask for forgiveness?
2. Why do you think forgiveness is such a big issue for people?
3. Do you find it easier to forgive a close friend or someone you hardly know?

Mark Tollefson

Chapter Twelve

STEP NINE
STOP BEING INFLUENCED BY
THE WORLD

As I look around at churches today and the Christians that fill those buildings I am greatly saddened by the way the world has influenced them. We have let the world both influence and in some cases dictate how we do church and what goes on inside the building. We have also let the world tell us the proper way to act and how we should live our lives. If you feel that I am exaggerating the point, just take some time to look at how the people in your church act and how the church is run as a whole. Now take a look at how the world runs its affairs at your place of employment. How much real difference do you see? How many similarities do you see between how non-Christians respond to each other and how we respond? Take a look at the values the world holds dear and you will see that many of those same values are in the church. This should not be. We are to show people how different life with Jesus is, we are not there to show them how close we are to the way the world acts. It is not simply that we are forgiven, it is that we have been changed.

I would like you to take some time and read 1 & 2 Corinthians. These letters were written to a church with issues. As you go through the various problems this young church was struggling with, you will see it is clear that the root cause of their struggles was allowing the world to influence them. Corinth was an area where many cultures and religions interacted with each other. Because of this the cultures and religions would affect each other. Maybe it would be better to say they would infect each other.

Many would take what they wanted from each culture and religion and merge it into some system they thought was convenient for them. We are of course in that same place now in our history in the western world. The Corinthian church was involved in sexual immorality, celebrity worship, obtaining their own rights over others, seeking the world's advice to solve problems within the body, using church for their own benefit, favouritism, to name a few. These were all done because they were contaminating the word of God with the world's ideas.

It is a shame that we today are in the exact same spot they were in that church. A while ago I was sitting in a restaurant in downtown Toronto with my pastor. We had a seat by the window and we were able to watch as people hurried by the window. My pastor had remarked how it was not too long ago we would have to send missionaries to reach many of the same people that were passing by the window as we sat and ate our dinner. Not only do we send missionaries but the world has come to this city. All different cultures and religions were right outside of that window and outside of the place you are sitting right now. What an opportunity we have to spread the gospel and allow Jesus to change people's lives.

The sad part is that those different cultures and religions seem at times to be influencing the church more than we are influencing them. Many Christians have done exactly what the early Greeks and Romans did in their time. We take some of their values and mix them in with what God has for us. This is never a good thing to do for Christians. We seem to think that by doing this we will be better able to reach these groups, but what really happens is that we become less and less like Jesus and more and more like the world.

We become just another option for the world to try instead of the only one that really works. Just look at one issue to see this play out. If you look it up, you will find that the number of failed marriages in the church is the same as in the world. We seem to be no different. Do you really think that you can live out the way of Jesus while mixing in some of the ways of the world.

Let us take a look at how the world has influenced us in the church. Sadly these are ways that the average Christian think are just fine. Our view of marriage is one. Most Christians will tell you that marriage is all about making you happy and this is what love is all about. They view love as something to make their life more joyous and happy. If you look at 1 Corinthians 13 to see what love looks like you will quickly see it has nothing to do with making us happy but everything to do with serving others. It is not about getting something for you but it is about giving to others. The world has told us, and Christians have embraced the doctrine about love being something we give to someone that makes us happy. There are many marriage seminars based on this theory. When we look to the author and finisher of our salvation to see how he demonstrated love. The love God has for us seems to be much different than what the modern church talks about. Jesus was not here to fulfill himself, His whole life was about fulfilling the mission of the Father.

The world tells us that if it makes you happy it must be good. The world operates on the premise that if it works for you it must be good. How many times have you heard that in the church? Sometimes it is as if the gospel was all about bringing us great happiness. Now of course when we properly follow Jesus by having a relationship with Him it will bring contentment and fulfillment but that is a by-product of a life lived for Him.

Of course this brings us to the "ME" generation that the world preaches. The world tells us it is all about us as individuals. Jesus tells us it is all about the Father. It is one way or the other. Unfortunately the church has tried to bring these two together and it has spelled trouble in the church. It seems today that Christians need to be continually recognized and validated for everything they do for God. The truth is, if you are seeking praise you are not really doing it for God you are doing it for yourself and your ego. It seems these days in churches we are constantly recognizing people for the great job they are doing. We seem to be fearful that if they do not get some sort of thanks they will stop doing ministry and the sad part is they may. If that is the reason they are doing ministry maybe they should not be doing it at all.

We have a culture of celebrity in the church much the same as the world does. The world has made heroes out of people that seem to have something that the average person does not have. It may be a singer, an actor, a politician or maybe a great business leader. While we at one time would not have idolized certain types of people in the general world we took the celebrity culture and ran with it.

What we did at first was we replaced those non-Christian celebrities with our own brand of Christian ones. We did it under the guise of being great examples. Now today we have celebrity pastors, singers, authors, etc. No longer do we want a pastor that just shepherds the flock, we want one that is exciting and has a big name in the world. We seem to quote those church celebrities more than we do the word of God. Now again some would say that this is okay. But of course we have now taken it to a new level, where not only do we crave the churches praise but now we want recognition from the world.

This is how it works when you bring a little of the world's thinking into the gospel. It immediately contaminates it and then destroys the message. Before you know it the message is not about Jesus it is about us. If you mix just a little anti-freeze in with your engine oil the damage will not be apparent right away. After time, as more gets mixed in, it will destroy everything.

We cannot live with one foot in the world and one foot with God. It cannot work. We need to realize that the world's way is wrong and sinful the end of which is death. When you look at Genesis three and see the damage that sin has done to the world why would you even think for a minute that mixing a little in with the church would be good.

"Your boasting is not good. Do you not know that a little leaven leavens the whole lump? Cleanse out the old leaven that you may be a new lump, as you really are unleavened. For Christ, our Passover lamb, has been sacrificed." (1

Corinthians 5:6-7)

"adulterous people! Do you not know that friendship with the world is enmity with God? Therefore whoever wishes to be a friend of the world makes himself an enemy of God." (James 4:4)

If we are going to live in the kingdom of God we have to stop looking to the world for our cues. We cannot love our enemies as Jesus commands, while believing the world that it is all about us. How can you love someone the way Jesus does when you are following the premise that your rights trumps others. No we can only truly love our enemy when we realize that our purpose in life is not to be happy. Our purpose is to direct others to the Father and make disciples. Happiness is the by-product not the product.

When we quote the verse that God will give us the desires of our heart we need to realize our hearts desires needs be about God not about our own selfish desires. In order to live out the fruit of the Spirit we need to crucify the works of the flesh. The only thing the world wants for us is to live out the works of the flesh. When we water down our lives by letting the world influence our behaviour we are really telling the world that a biblical worldview is not enough we need add-ons. I am here to tell you that the gospel is complete it needs nothing the world has to offer. In fact anything the world has to offer will only take away from the gospel and rob us of the joy that serving Jesus provides for us. Jesus proved this by coming to earth and living out this life without sin or contamination from the world.

Remember 1 Peter 1:3.

"His divine power has granted to us all things that pertain to life and godliness, through the knowledge of him who called us to his own glory and excellence,"

Questions

1. Think of one area of your life where you have taken more of your cues from the world instead of scripture.
2. When we have the Bible to read and we can look back at history to see the end result of what happens when we mix the world's thinking with God's way why do we still think it is a good idea to mix the two together?
3. In your experience what are some of the ways the church has been influenced by the world's thinking?

Chronic Christian

CHAPTER THIRTEEN

STEP TEN
CONTINUE IN THE APOSTLES
DOCTRINE

*"And they devoted themselves to the apostles'
teaching and the fellowship, to the breaking of
bread and the prayers." (Acts 2:42)*

When we talk about the apostles doctrine we are
simply talking about the Word of God. We are
talking about the way God wants us to live our life
in a world that does not know Him. The early
Christians were convicted of their sinful selves so
they repented and were baptized and then continued
on in the faith. We seem to have some people today
that simply ask for forgiveness, acknowledge Jesus
as saviour and then go on with their lives as if
nothing happened. Whatever doctrine they were
following before they just seem to carry on with
that and then they wonder why there is no change in
their lives. If we are going to live this life in the

manner that Jesus did we need to continue living in the word not in the world.

This is more than just having a head knowledge of God's word. It is not just an intellectual assent to His word but it is actually living it out in our day to day lives. We cannot expect to have a victorious Christian life unless we continue in the Word. There are those that will act like Jesus was just added to something they already had. When I talk about continuing in something I mean we are daily being intentional about following the way of Jesus. It is not something that just happens by accident. It takes us to get up every day and intend to be steadfast in our walk.

When one is married, if they do not continually follow what we might call the rules of marriage, they will have problems from the beginning. If you do not get up every day and live out the reality of being married then you will not be able to keep those vows. We need to wake up every morning intending to work on our relationship with our spouse so that we can maintain it and improve it continually. If we do not have that attitude our relationship will soon turn into something we do not want. A good marriage relationship does not happen by accident. We must continue in the marriage relationship and continue to go deeper in that relationship with our spouse. It is the same way with our relationship with Jesus.

Most people, when they first start to follow Jesus,

are very committed to listening to and doing all that He has laid out for them. The problem comes in as we walk with Jesus for a while. We tend to become more casual in our commitment. It is not necessarily that we do not believe or that we do not want to follow His ways. But we let the cares and the beliefs of this world affect how we view Jesus. When this happens to us we need to be very careful and return to the biblical truths.

Continuing in the apostles doctrine is consistently and continually doing what Jesus told us to do. It is not good enough to follow the Spirit fifty percent of the time. It is a one hundred percent commitment. Some Christians seem to follow the way of Jesus when in their minds it seems to work out the way they expected. Or maybe just when it is convenient. There cannot be times when we respond the world's way, and then some times we respond the Christian way. When the world sees us doing that we are really telling them that following Jesus only works for some of the areas of our life.

Some people feel that if they follow the apostles doctrine for some things they will still get some benefit. The truth is that this is an all or nothing commitment. There are letters written in the Bible to churches that have lost their steadfastness and have tried to return to their old ways. In their minds they were not giving up on the faith but they just added some old ways back into what they believed. In every instance it led to them falling away and they had to be called back to Jesus. If we are going to win this race we need to continue in the teachings of scripture and no others. We cannot mix anything else in with them, it only contaminates our relationship with Jesus. Of course we can only do this if we know those teachings.

When we let ourselves drift from the apostles doctrines this is when false teachers and false doctrine thrive. There are many people that would call themselves Christians but they are ignorant to the beliefs in the Bible. They may even refer to themselves as followers of Christ but at the same time they have no real idea of what He taught and is recorded in scripture. They will make all kinds of excuses of why they are unaware and sadly church leaders will not call them to a higher standard. Part of the reason that the leaders do not expect the average Christian to know much about doctrine is because many of them have no idea about it either. In many cases we have church leaders that have never been taught to study the scripture. If they do not know the Bible how would we expect them to be able to teach it to us.

How can we expect to live out kingdom principles when we do not know what they are? If I was to take someone off the street and put them in the cockpit of an airplane, then expect them to be able to fly it without training, you would find that laughable. They may even be able to figure out how to start the engines and maybe even get it to move but the end result would be disastrous. In the same manner, we should not expect to be able to live out our calling as Jesus' followers, if we do not know and continue in the teachings of the Bible. It is not enough to just know them, but we have to be consistent in putting them into action. If you know how to drive a car, but never drive, you will not be very good at it and that knowledge will not do you much good.

You have heard the old saying that practice makes perfect. That statement applies to our walk with Jesus as well. If we continue to persevere in the teachings of scripture it will become easier for us to live out. We all know that if we have a bad habit it become an automatic response. In the same way when we constantly live out the way of Jesus it becomes second nature to us. At some point it becomes our first response not our last. I like to say that good habits are still habits.

Most people have more knowledge about their favourite pastime than they do about the Bible. How many sports fans can quote statistics till it makes you dizzy? How many Christians know more about celebrities than they do about the people in the Bible? Some will even defend it by saying the people they know so much about are Christians. We need to get back to our first love and continue in the apostles doctrine. There is no other way for this to work. If you are in school, you concentrate on what you are learning so you can pass the coming tests. We have a test coming also, and that test happens every day. It involves the way we react to the everyday situations of life. We will only pass by responding in the way Jesus wants us to act and then draw people to Him. Or we will respond the way the world tells us to respond and turn people away from the Father and fail the test. Let us keep studying to pass the test.

"Do your best to present yourself to God as one approved, a worker who has no need to be ashamed, rightly handling the word of truth". (2 Timothy 2:15)

Questions

1. If you were to be really honest with yourself what do you know more about, your favourite pastime or TV show or the things of God?
2. What is one area of scripture that you know you are not completely following as you should?
3. Why do you not follow that area of scripture that you answered in question 2?

Mark Tollefson

CHAPTER FOURTEEN

STEP ELEVEN
MAINTIAN A HEALTHY
SPIRITUAL LIFE

"For where your treasure is, there your heart will be also". (Matthew 6:21)

I want you to take some time to think about how much time you spend doing different activities in your life. Look at how much time you spend at work, taking the kids to different events, watching television, listening to music, on the internet, reading books or whatever it is you think you need to do daily. Now look at the amount of time you spend in God's word each day or how much time you spend in prayer. Or how much time you spend working on your relationship with Jesus.

If you are like most Christians you spend most of your day doing the mundane things of life or chasing after some dream. You have convinced yourself that the time you spend in leisure is time you have earned because of the busy life you lead. You will probably see that you spend very little time working on your relationship with Jesus. At the same time you like to tell everyone it is not about religion it is about relationship. If that were really true in your life do you not think you would spend more time working on that relationship than you do right now? Do you really think that you can live a victorious Christian life when instead of maintaining a healthy spiritual life you spend more time maintaining what the world told you is important?

"Have nothing to do with irreverent, silly myths. Rather train yourself for godliness;" (1 Timothy 4:7)

Nobody wakes up one day to find out they are an Olympic athlete. You may wake up one day and make a commitment to become one but it does not just happen. Once you have decided that you have a particular talent in a sport it takes commitment, discipline and sacrifice to achieve your goal. You will need to gain knowledge about your particular event. It cannot be just a passing knowledge you will need to know all the finer points of the skill to perform at that level. It will take much discipline for the hours of training ahead of you. You will have to sacrifice your own wants along the way to be able to spend the time necessary to reach the prize. If you are one of the few that will one day stand on the podium with a gold medal around your neck I am sure you will think it was all worthwhile. Even though it is fleeting and the next time around many will have forgotten about you as they crown a new champion.

In the same way we as Christians need to maintain a healthy spiritual life. There are times it will take sacrifice but it is well worth the effort. It will take discipline and it will take us to be intentional about what we are doing and keeping our focus. A healthy spiritual life is not something that just happens, it takes effort. I know that it is Jesus that provides us with the power to actually live out our calling but unless we spend time using that power in our lives it will not do us much good. It is gas that gives a car the power to drive but unless we put that gas in the car it will go nowhere. Once we have the gas, we need to keep our cars well maintained to get the peak performance out of them. We can ignore the maintenance of the vehicle and it may keep running for a while but it will not run at its best and eventually it will break down.

We need to realize that we need to work at our Christian walk daily. We need to do things that will enhance our walk and help us to be more like Jesus.

"You therefore, beloved, knowing this beforehand, take care that you are not carried away with the error of lawless people and lose your own stability. But grow in the grace and knowledge of our Lord and Savior Jesus Christ. To him be the glory both

now and to the day of eternity. Amen." (2 Peter 3:17-18)

We can see that we are called to grow in The Lord. We are not to stay in the same place spiritually as we were when He first called us to Himself. The question becomes what kind of things can we do to maintain a spiritually healthy life. The fact is there have been books written on this subject but I would like to just look at a few areas of our lives we can make changes to so that we can become healthy.

The first place to start is the most obvious. Christians need to spend more time in Bible study. We have talked about this is a previous step but it does not hurt to be reminded again. When I say Bible study I am talking about more than just a ten minute devotion each morning. A quick read of scripture each day is important and very useful in our walk, but we also need to take time to really study the scriptures. Most people shy away from this simply because they feel it is too difficult. There are two reasons for this happening. First they do not want to spend the time it takes or secondly they may just not know how to do it.

As for the time issue remember the opening paragraph. We have time to do what we feel is important for us. The higher amount of importance we put on an activity the more time we will make for it. It is amazing that most Christians have time for their favourite television program but they cannot make time for Bible study. Maybe we should say they will make time for what they want to do or what will entertain them. It is sad that most midweek Bible studies are attended by very few Christians.

If you are one of those people that really do not know how to study the Bible then it is time for that to change. We cannot afford to sit back thinking that because we do not know how to do it we can ignore it. Have someone teach you how to study the Bible. This can be a challenge at times because churches have not done a very good job equipping the people sitting in the pews to study scripture. We spend more time feeding people then we do teaching them how to eat. Thankfully there are good resources out there to teach you this skill. Make no mistake, Bible study is a skill. Take the time to learn the skill and you will be amazed what treasures you will find in the word of God.

Prayer is another one those spiritual disciplines that will help us to live the way of Jesus. Our everyday relationships would not be healthy if we did not communicate with each other. So why is it we think we can follow Jesus without spending time with Him? Many of us will make a list of requests of things for Him to do but it needs to be more than that. Paul tells us in 1 Thessalonians 5:17 *"to pray without ceasing".* This is a life of constant communion with our Lord. Some Christians have a particular time of day to pray, a time they lay out their requests and questions to God. There is nothing wrong with you having a consistent time every day to pray, in fact you should have that time. But we should not limit our prayer life to just those times. We can talk to Him whenever we want throughout the day.

The other mistake we tend to make in our prayer life is to try to hide things from God. Somehow we forget that He already knows them. We just need to be honest with Him. Tell Him what we are feeling and ask for His help to work through the issues of life. As you read through the Bible and look at the great men of God, you quickly see that they were very honest with God about their feelings. It was not that they did not have great respect for God but they told Him how they felt and He responded. He may not always respond how we think that He should, but He can certainly handle our tough questions. The problem only comes when we fail to accept the answers.

Fellowship is another big part of our spiritual health. We have talked earlier about accountability but that is just one of the aspect of fellowship that is important. Now I am not telling you that all your friends have to be Christian and we need to only hang out with other Christians. In fact we need to interact with the world. But it is important to have the fellowship of other believers.

When we gather together we need to be able to encourage one another on this walk with Jesus. We need that support from each other. We need to challenge each other.

"Rejoice with those who rejoice, weep with those who weep.' (Romans 12:15)

We need to know we are not on this journey alone. When we fellowship with each other it will also give us a chance to talk about the things of The Lord. This is important because a big part of our lives are spent at our jobs in the world and we will be talking about anything but God. It is refreshing to be reminded of the blessings of God by your friends. It will give you a chance to ask each other questions and go deeper with The Lord. This does not happen when you are talking about the latest sporting event with your partner at work.

There is a place for both conversations. Even when you are talking about everyday things with your Christian brothers and sisters you are still looking at it with a biblical world view. This helps in your battle with the flesh because as you discuss the issues of life you will be encouraged to react the way Jesus would. When you tell your non-Christian friends about someone that has wronged you they respond from a worldly perspective and as you keep hearing the wrong way you may at some point be convinced they are right.

When it comes to spiritual discipline I need to talk about how we entertain ourselves. Most Christian will spend some of their time listening to music, watching television, reading books, playing video games or on the internet. I would say that the majority of Christians spend most of the time they spend on entertainment consuming secular entertainment. What I mean by the term secular entertainment is any product that promotes worldly thinking as being the norm. The main message is what the flesh desires. This can be both overt and covertly done. For instance, there are many musical acts that on the surface seem to be presenting a neutral message but in fact they are still worldly messages. They may seem to be innocent but they are not calling us to live as God intended. Then there is the type of entertainment that is very overt about its message. As you evaluate your choices keep this verse in mind.

"Whoever is not with me is against me, and whoever does not gather with me scatters." (Matthew 12:30)

Now I am not saying that one should never take in secular entertainment. But what I am saying is that if that is all you are ever exposed to then you will have a difficult, if not impossible, time living your life the way Jesus lived while He was on earth.

"Do not be conformed to this world, but be transformed by the renewal of your mind, that by testing you may discern what is the will of God, what is good and acceptable and perfect."(Romans 12:2)

We cannot renew our minds when all our time is spent filling it with the things of this world. If the only time you spend renewing your mind with the things of God is one hour on Sunday then you will not be able to live out your calling successfully. There need to be times when instead of reading the latest novel you should do a Bible Study or read a book about our faith. When was the last time you were on YouTube and instead of looking up the latest video you watched a sermon. When it comes to music, how much of the music you listen to has a Christian message as opposed to the world's message we are bombarded with daily? When was the last time when you were in the car alone you turned off the radio and talked to God?

When we never spend time with the things of The Lord or His people it will damage our spiritual health. What we put into our minds and hearts will determine how we behave. Have you ever been around really negative people? After a while you will find if you are not practising spiritual disciplines you will be more like them then they are like you. You may think that you can constantly take in the world's message without it harming you but that is just not true. Because we live in the world, but we are not of this world, we need to spend time in activities that reinforce Godly behaviour so we can withstand the pressure of the world to be like them. We can rise above the world's message while being here because of Jesus, but like the runner training for a race we need to train to live the kingdom life. I will end this step with this passage from Philippians because it speaks for itself.

"Finally, brothers, whatever is true, whatever is honorable, whatever is just, whatever is pure, whatever is lovely, whatever is commendable, if there is any excellence, if there is anything worthy of praise, think about these things." (Philippians 4:8)

Questions

1. List the activities you are involved in that help you maintain a healthy spiritual life.
2. Which of the items on your list seem to give you the most benefit?
3. What are some areas in your life that are harming your spiritual life in Jesus?

Chronic Christian

CHAPTER FIFTEEN

STEP TWELVE
SPREAD THE GOOD NEWS OF
THE KINGDOM

"And Jesus came and said to them, "All authority in heaven and on earth has been given to me. Go therefore and make disciples of all nations, baptizing them in the name of the Father and of the Son and of the Holy Spirit, teaching them to observe all that I have commanded you. And behold, I am with you always, to the end of the age." (Matthew 28:18-20)

There is really no way Jesus could have made our mission clearer. As He was about to ascend to the Father this was His command to His disciples. We are to go about making disciples. Our goal on this earth is not to be happy or wealthy or healthy, you may get some of these, but our whole goal of this life is to make disciples. We are not to live out kingdom principles so that people will look at and notice us. It is all about bringing people to Jesus. It is all about building up the kingdom of God. As we looked at earlier in this book, the kingdom is both here and in the future.

"In the same way, let your light shine before others, so that they may see your good works and give glory to your Father who is in heaven." (Matthew 5:16)

This final step is not something new I am introducing to you. In fact this is not even an option if we are following Jesus. Our whole lives need to be about this ministry. When we take a look at the gospels and the life that Jesus led here on earth we quickly see that this was the entire focus of His journey here. It is interesting that we only see the last few years of His life as the ministry part. We feel this is the only time He was about the Fathers work but that is just not true. He spent the first part of His earthly life preparing for the last years of what we think of as the ministry part. When He was twelve this is what He told His mother about what He was doing when they had lost track of Him.

"And he said to them, "Why were you looking for me? Did you not know that I must be in my Father's house?" And they did not understand the saying that he spoke to them. And they did not understand the saying that he spoke to them. And Jesus increased in wisdom and in stature and in favor with God and man." (Luke 2:49-52)

Here He is, as a twelve year old, knowing full well what His mission was. How many twelve year olds do you know with this much focus. As He went about His life until His public ministry He was being prepared for that task. He was setting the example by living a life the way God intended for us to live. When He did start His public ministry the people around Him had already been watching Him and knew how He lived. So we should never look at any aspect of our lives other than being a ministry. We are to fulfill this mission whatever stage of life we are in. We need to keep focused on God's mission. Even at those times you cannot see that God is using you directly He is doing a work in your life.

Aside from this being a command, and aside from the fact that by following our orders we are helping to rescue people from an eternity of separation from God in Hell. There are benefits to us when it comes to our walk with Jesus and living out the Spirit led life.

The first benefit we see comes in our ability to better focus on being led by the Spirit. We need to keep in mind that how we live says a lot about God and that is who we are trying to introduce to people.

"Therefore, we are ambassadors for Christ, God making his appeal through us. We implore you on behalf of Christ, be reconciled to God." (2 Corinthians 5:20)

When a person is an ambassador for a country everything they say and do reflects on who they are representing. If they do something negative it will make people look on that country in a bad light. It may even keep people from wanting to visit that country. Likewise if they do something that is quite remarkable it will make people stand up and take notice. It will leave people with a good feeling toward that country. In the same way when we are telling people about Jesus or even if they just know that we are Christians what we do reflects on Jesus. How many times have you heard people comment about the actions someone did that was supposed to be a Christian. It goes something like this "that guy claims to be Christian but do you see how he treats his wife".

Although the world will always find something in our lives they think is not good we should not give them a reason to find fault with Jesus. When we keep in our mind the fact that it is our job to make disciples it will help remind us that we are an example for God. It will help us to think before we act. We will start to consider how our actions or our reactions will reflect on the message we are trying to share with others. When you are at work you are always aware of what you are doing in case the boss is looking. We need to have that same awareness because the world is watching what we are doing. We do not want to hurt our testimony and make it more difficult to bring glory to the Father. So when we preach the good news of the kingdom we will be so aware of our witness it will help us to live out the Spirit filled life.

The next benefit of sharing the good news with others is that it help builds our faith and we are able to learn more about God as we share with others. It will help to build our faith because as we become more intentional about making disciples we will become more dependent on God. The fact is that you cannot make disciples without the help of the Holy Spirit. So as we see the Spirit move in our lives and in others it will automatically build our faith even more. There are many times that as you share with others it will actually do you more good than it will do for them if they do not accept the truth.

As you are sharing your faith and your walk with others they will ask questions and some of them you will not have a good answer for. This will make it so you will have to go back and search the scriptures to get a better understanding of the issue raised. As you do this you will learn more and it will deepen your relationship with Jesus. You do not need to feel like you need to have all the answers before you disciple others. What you do need is the commitment to the process. We need to realize that no matter how long we have been in this relationship with Jesus that there will be questions we do not have a good answer for and that is okay. That is why how we live our life is so important. People will be able to stump you with a hard question or they can always argue and not accept what you are saying. But they cannot deny the way you are living your life. They may think that it is crazy to love your enemy but they will know if you are living out that reality in your day to day life.

The fact that Jesus left us with the job of making disciples is not an accident. It is not simply that He had no other way of doing it. He knew the benefit we would get out of the whole process. He knew it would help us to live out our calling in Him. Jesus calls us to Himself through others and then He uses us to call others and then as we grow in our faith we disciple other people. As we disciple other people we will grow in our relationship with Him. And as we disciple people the ones we disciple are supposed to be working on the same mission. And on and on it goes. And yes He did set it up that way on purpose.

Remember that not only is this step twelve of this program but it is part of God's overall plan of redemption for mankind. It is a command and it is not just a good suggestion. Many times we hear people say that the Bible is a good way to live your life but it is not for them. It is not just a good idea it is the only one that actually works.

When He told Peter to feed his sheep He knew all along that Peter would as well be fed as He fed others. If you have a family and you are making dinner for them it is rare that you would make them a big meal and not eat yourself. As your family is getting full, you are getting full. So let us get out there and be about making disciples that make disciples. Let us reap the benefits of the process.

Questions

1. Why are we hesitant to spread the good news?
2. Think of one time that you did spread the good news of Jesus and you really saw a benefit to you?
3. Do you find it a privilege or a chore to be part of God's plan of reconciliation by sharing the good news?

Chronic Christian

CHAPTER 16

Conclusion

So here we are at the end of the book which is really the beginning for us. As we walk along this journey I need to remind you of a few thoughts.

I do not want to leave you with the impression that you go through these steps once and it is all done and you never have to do them again. The steps are not a magical formula that once you have done once make you immune to the enemy. These are steps you need to live out daily in your life. The battle does not end till Jesus returns and judgement happens. Then there will be a new heaven and earth and all will be completely renewed and set right.

This is a daily battle with the flesh nature. If we realize every morning that we are in a battle we will realize that not a day will go by that we do not need our armour. As we put these steps into play it will become more natural for us and the victories will just keep coming. As soon as we forget that we are in a battle that is when the enemy will sneak up and attack you. He wants to catch you off guard.

We do not need to be fearful of the battle. We have been given the necessary tools to win. God has not given us a Spirit of fear.

"For you did not receive the spirit of slavery to fall back into fear, but you have received the Spirit of adoption as sons, by whom we cry, "Abba! Father!"(Romans 8:15)

We do not need to fear the battle but we do need to be aware of what is going on. If you were fighting in a war in a foreign land you would not think of going into battle without your weapons. So as we go into each day let us go prepared to win the war in the power of God.

"Now to him who is able to do far more abundantly than all that we ask or think, according to the power at work within us, to him be glory in the church and in Christ Jesus throughout all generations, forever and ever. Amen." (Ephesians 3:20-21)

Lastly this Christian life is not just a life of self-denial and rules. When we live life the way God intended, it is a life that is difficult to even put into words. When we really get a hold of who God is and what He wants for us we will truly have the abundant life that Jesus came to provide for us. Our joy and contentment will not be dictated by our surroundings and our stuff. Our joy will come from the creator of all. We will truly have the peace that is without explanation.

"And the peace of God, which surpasses all understanding, will guard your hearts and your minds in Christ Jesus." (Philippians 4:7)

Questions
1. Will you commit to living out kingdom principles every day?
2. Do you want the abundant life that Jesus came to provide or are you satisfied with what the world has to offer?

Join us on Facebook at
https://www.facebook.com/chronicchrist
ian?ref=hl

Email the author at
kingdomlivingguy@gmail.com